Guilt-Free Sweet Treats

Guilt-Free Sweet Treats

DELICIOUS 300-CALORIE-OR-LESS DESSERTS

Woman's Day

First published in 2010 in the United States of America by Filipacchi Publishing
1633 Broadway
New York, NY 10019

Woman's Day is a registered trademark of Hachette Filipacchi Media U.S., Inc.

DESIGN: Rita Sowins / Sowins Design
EDITOR: Lauren Kuczala
PRODUCTION: Lynn Scaglione and Annie Andres

ISBN-13: 978-1-933231-73-0
Library of Congress Control Number: 2009938282

Printed in China

contents

bars

Brownies

PLANNING TIP:
Store airtight at cool room
temperature up to 3 days.

FYI: These are more fudgy than cakey.

1 stick (½ cup) butter
4 oz unsweetened baking chocolate,
   chopped
1⅓ cups sugar
3 large eggs
1½ tsp vanilla extract
¾ cup all-purpose flour

1. Heat oven to 350°F. Line an 8-in. square baking pan with foil, letting ends extend above pan on opposite sides. Coat foil with nonstick spray.
2. Melt butter and chocolate in a medium saucepan over low heat; stir until blended. Off heat, whisk in sugar, then eggs, 1 at a time. Stir in vanilla and flour.
3. Spread in prepared pan. Bake 25 to 30 minutes until a wooden pick inserted in center comes out with moist crumbs attached.
4. Cool in pan on a wire rack. Lift foil by ends to cutting board. Cut into 16 squares.

PER BROWNIE: 189 CAL • 3 G PRO • 23 G CAR • 1 G FIBER • 11 G FAT (6 G SAT FAT) • 55 MG CHOL • 72 MG SOD

Snickers Brownie Bites

MAKES 42 / ACTIVE: 30 MIN
TOTAL: 1½ HR

1 stick (½ cup) butter
4 oz unsweetened baking chocolate
1⅓ cups sugar
3 large eggs
1½ tsp vanilla extract
¾ cup all-purpose flour
1 bag (13 oz) Snickers Mini candy bars
¼ cup M&M's mini–baking bits

1. Heat oven to 350°F. Line miniature muffin pan(s) with paper liners. (Cups measure 1¼ in. across bottom.)
2. Melt butter and chocolate in a medium saucepan over low heat or in a large bowl in microwave. Stir to blend well.
3. Whisk in sugar, eggs and vanilla until combined. Stir in flour just until blended.
4. Spoon 1 measuring tablespoon batter into each muffin cup. Press in a Snickers bar almost flush with surface; sprinkle with 4 or 5 baking bits.
5. Bake 16 to 18 minutes until risen and tops look dry and shiny (some may have caramel flow). Cool in pan on a wire rack 5 minutes; remove from pan, using tip of a knife if needed, to rack to cool completely. Repeat with remaining batter.

PER BROWNIE: 120 CAL • 2 G PRO • 15 G CAR • 1 G FIBER • 7 G FAT (3 G SAT FAT) • 22 MG CHOL • 49 MG SOD

Triple Chocolate Mousse Pyramids

MAKES 42 / ACTIVE: 30 MIN
TOTAL: 1½ HR
(PLUS 2 HR CHILLING)

PLANNING TIP:
Can be made up to 3 days ahead.
Refrigerate covered.

COOKIE CRUST
1 cup all-purpose flour
⅔ cup Dutch process unsweetened
   cocoa powder
1 stick (½ cup) butter, softened
1 cup confectioners' sugar
1 large egg yolk
½ tsp vanilla extract

MOUSSE
1½ cups heavy (whipping) cream
¼ cup granulated sugar
1 tsp vanilla extract
1 bag (11.5 oz) milk-chocolate chips
4 large eggs

MARBLED GLAZE
½ oz semisweet baking chocolate,
   very finely chopped
8 oz white baking chocolate
2 Tbsp solid vegetable shortening

1. Heat oven to 350°F. Line a 13 x 9 x 2-in. baking pan with nonstick foil, letting foil extend about 2 in. above ends of pan.
2. CRUST: Whisk flour and cocoa in a small bowl to blend. In a large bowl, beat butter, confectioners' sugar, egg yolk and vanilla with mixer on medium speed, scraping down sides of bowl as needed, 1 to 2 minutes until fluffy. On low speed, add flour mixture. Beat 1 minute or until moist clumps form. Scatter over bottom of prepared pan; press into an even layer. Bake 11 minutes or until crust puffs and looks dry and set. Place pan on a wire rack.
3. MOUSSE: While crust bakes, stir cream, sugar and vanilla in a 1-qt microwave-safe measure or bowl to blend; add chocolate. Microwave on high 2 to 3 minutes until cream barely starts to simmer. Whisk until chocolate melts and mixture is smooth. Cool 8 minutes. Whisk in eggs, 1 at a time, until blended. Pour over hot crust.
4. Bake 30 to 32 minutes until edges have risen slightly higher than center (middle will be set, but soft).
5. GLAZE: Meanwhile, seal semisweet chocolate in a small, sturdy ziptop bag. Place in a small bowl of hot tap water. Let sit, squeezing bag a few times, until chocolate melts, adding hot water if needed. Melt white chocolate and shortening in a small saucepan over low heat. Stir until smooth.
6. Pour white chocolate over hot mousse; spread evenly. Dry bag of chocolate, snip tip off a corner and pipe thin lines and squiggles over white chocolate. Draw a wooden pick through semisweet chocolate to marbleize. Refrigerate uncovered 2 hours until Glaze hardens.
7. Holding foil ends, lift to a cutting board. With a knife dipped in warm water, and using a gentle sawing motion, carefully cut crosswise into 6 strips. Cut each strip into 7 triangles. Refrigerate.

PER PYRAMID: 167 CAL • 2 G PRO • 16 G CAR • 0 G FIBER • 11 G FAT (6 G SAT FAT) • 45 MG CHOL • 50 MG SOD

Sweet & Salty
Pretzel Brownies

1⅓ cups (8 oz) semisweet chocolate chips

4 oz unsweetened baking chocolate, coarsely chopped

1 stick (½ cup) unsalted butter

61 saltine crackers, finely crushed

1 can (14 oz) fat-free sweetened condensed milk (not evaporated milk)

3 cups bite-size pretzels

1. Line a 9-in. square baking pan with nonstick foil, letting foil extend about 2 in. above opposite ends of pan.

2. Melt both chocolates and the butter in a large bowl in microwave or in a heavy saucepan over medium-low heat, stirring often, until blended and smooth. Remove from heat; stir in cracker crumbs (you should have 2 cups) and milk until blended. Fold in 2 cups pretzels.

3. Spread evenly in prepared pan. Lay remaining pretzels on top. Cover and refrigerate at least 1½ hours or until firm.

4. Lift foil by ends onto cutting board. Cut into 6 strips, then cut each strip into 6 squares.

PER SQUARE: 136 CAL • 2 G PRO • 18 G CAR • 1 G FIBER • 7 G FAT (4 G SAT FAT) • 9 MG CHOL • 138 MG SOD

Mocha Cheesecake Bars

MAKES 48 / ACTIVE: 18 MIN
TOTAL: AT LEAST 4 HR
(INCLUDES CHILLING TIME)

CRUST

30 reduced-fat chocolate sandwich
cookies (such as Oreos)

¼ cup fat-free bottled hot fudge
topping, not heated

1 envelope unflavored gelatin

½ cup cold strong coffee

2 bricks (8 oz each) ⅓-less-fat cream
cheese (Neufchâtel), softened

¾ cup sugar

1 cup (8 oz) reduced-fat sour cream

1 bar (3 oz) bittersweet chocolate,
broken up and melted

GARNISH: chocolate-covered coffee
beans

1. Line a 13 x 9-in. baking pan with nonstick foil, letting foil extend about 2 in. above narrow ends of pan.
2. CRUST: Pulse cookies in food processor until fine crumbs form. Add fudge topping to crumbs; pulse to moisten. Press firmly in bottom of prepared pan. Freeze while proceeding.
3. Sprinkle gelatin over coffee in a small saucepan; let stand 2 minutes. Stir over low heat until steaming and granules dissolve. Remove from heat.
4. Beat cream cheese and sugar in a large bowl with mixer on high speed until smooth. On low speed, beat in sour cream, the coffee mixture and chocolate until blended. Pour onto crust, cover and refrigerate 4 hours or until firm.
5. Lift foil by ends onto cutting board. Cut crosswise into 8 strips, then cut each strip into 6 bars. Add coffee beans to top.

PER BAR: 84 CAL • 2 G PRO • 11 G CAR • 0 G FIBER • 4 G FAT (2 G SAT FAT) • 8 MG CHOL • 88 MG SOD

Sweetie Swirl Cheesecake Bars

MAKES 32 / ACTIVE: 30 MIN
TOTAL: 1 HR (PLUS COOLING
AND CHILLING)

PLANNING TIP:
Refrigerate bars airtight with wax paper between layers up to 1 week or freeze up to 3 months.

CRUST
1½ sticks (¾ cup) butter, softened
1 cup confectioners' sugar
½ tsp salt
1½ cups all-purpose flour

FILLING
4 oz white baking chocolate
1 cup frozen unsweetened raspberries, thawed
2 bricks (8 oz each) cream cheese, softened
½ cup granulated sugar
2 large eggs
½ cup sour cream
1 tsp vanilla extract
2 Tbsp all-purpose flour
¼ tsp each liquid red food color and raspberry extract

1. Heat oven to 325°F. Line a 13 x 9-in. baking pan with foil, letting foil extend about 2 in. above ends of pan.
2. CRUST: Beat butter in a medium bowl with mixer on medium-high speed until creamy. Add confectioners' sugar and salt; beat 1 minute until light and fluffy. On low speed, gradually beat in flour just until blended. With fingers, press evenly over bottom of pan.
3. Bake 18 minutes or until golden. Place pan on a wire rack; let cool.
4. FILLING: Melt chocolate in a small bowl in microwave as package directs. Cool to room temperature.
5. Meanwhile, with a rubber spatula, press raspberries through a fine strainer set over a medium bowl (you should have ¼ cup purée); discard seeds.
6. Beat cream cheese and granulated sugar in a large bowl with mixer on medium-high speed 2 minutes or until creamy. On low speed, beat in eggs, 1 at a time, until combined. Beat in sour cream and vanilla extract, then flour just until blended.
7. Stir 1 cup batter, the food color and raspberry extract into raspberry purée; remove and reserve ½ cup. Stir melted white chocolate into remaining batter. Pour 1½ cups white batter over crust; top with spoonfuls of remaining raspberry mixture, then remaining white batter to cover. Top with small dollops reserved raspberry mixture. Drag a toothpick through dollops and white batter to marbleize.
8. Bake 32 to 35 minutes until slightly puffed and set. Cool completely in pan on a wire rack, then refrigerate at least 1 hour until firm.
9. TO SERVE: Holding foil by ends, lift to cutting board. Cut into 4 equal rows lengthwise and 8 crosswise.

PER BAR: 172 CAL • 3 G PRO • 15 G CAR • 0 G FIBER • 11 G FAT (7 G SAT FAT) • 43 MG CHOL • 132 MG SOD

Key Lime Bars

CRUST
35 reduced-fat vanilla wafer cookies
2 Tbsp each confectioners' sugar and
    sweetened flaked coconut
2 Tbsp light butter

TOPPING
3 large egg whites
2 large eggs
1½ cups granulated sugar
3 Tbsp all-purpose flour
1 tsp baking powder
1½ tsp grated Key lime or regular
    lime zest
½ cup fresh Key lime or regular lime
    juice
Confectioners' sugar for dusting
GARNISH: thin strips lime zest

1. CRUST: Heat oven to 350°F. Line a 9-in. square baking pan with nonstick foil. In food processor, pulse cookies, sugar and coconut until cookies are reduced to fine crumbs. Add butter; pulse until mixture is damp. Press crumb mixture evenly and firmly over bottom of prepared pan; bake 10 minutes or until crust is set and pale golden.

2. TOPPING: While crust bakes, in a 2-qt glass measure or bowl, whisk egg whites, whole eggs and sugar until combined. Add remaining ingredients; whisk until well blended. Pour egg mixture onto hot crust and return to oven. Continue to bake 30 minutes or until topping is pale golden and just set.

3. Remove pan to wire rack. Immediately loosen edges with tip of knife where topping meets foil. Let cool completely. Refrigerate 1 hour.

4. To serve, lift from pan by foil and transfer to cutting board. Cut into 16 squares. Dust with confectioners' sugar and top with zest.

PER BAR: 143 CAL • 2 G PRO • 29 G CAR • 0 G FIBER • 3 G FAT (1 G SAT FAT) • 28 MG CHOL • 99 MG SOD

Raspberry-Blueberry Cake

MAKES 24 / ACTIVE: 15 MIN
TOTAL: 50 MIN

PLANNING TIP:
Can be refrigerated covered up to
1 week.

Basic Batter (see recipe, below)
1 Tbsp grated lemon zest
1 cup each fresh raspberries and
   blueberries
GARNISH: confectioners' sugar

1. Heat oven to 350°F. Line a 13 x 9 x 2-in. baking pan with nonstick foil, letting foil extend above sides of pan.
2. Prepare Basic Batter, adding the lemon zest. Spread evenly in prepared pan. Scatter berries over top.
3. Bake 35 minutes or until a wooden pick inserted in center comes out clean. Cool in pan on a wire rack. Holding edges of foil, lift cake from pan. Dust with confectioners' sugar. Cut into 2-in. squares.

Basic Batter

1½ sticks (¾ cup) unsalted butter, softened
1½ cups sugar
2 tsp each baking powder and vanilla extract
4 large eggs
2¼ cups all-purpose flour
1 cup milk

1. Beat butter, sugar, baking powder and vanilla in a large bowl with mixer on high 3 minutes or until fluffy.
2. Add eggs, 1 at a time, beating well after each. On low speed, beat in flour in 3 additions alternately with milk in 2 additions, just until blended, scraping sides of bowl as needed.

PER SQUARE: 169 CAL • 3 G PRO • 24 G CAR • 1 G FIBER • 7 G FAT (4 G SAT FAT) • 52 MG CHOL • 59 MG SOD

Almond Triangles

MAKES 48 / ACTIVE: 20 MIN
TOTAL: 55 MIN

⅔ cup sugar

⅛ tsp ground cinnamon

2½ cups all-purpose flour

¼ tsp salt

2 sticks (1 cup) cold unsalted butter,
   cut up

2 large eggs, yolk and white separated,
   whites slightly beaten

1 tsp almond extract

⅔ cup sliced almonds

1. Heat oven to 350°F. Line a 13 x 9-in. baking pan with nonstick foil, letting foil extend about 2 in. above pan on two sides.

2. Mix 1 Tbsp sugar and the cinnamon in a small bowl. Set aside.

3. In a food processor, pulse remaining sugar, the flour and salt until blended. Add butter and pulse until mixture resembles coarse crumbs. Add yolks and extract, and pulse just until mixed.

4. Press dough into pan. Brush with egg white until moistened (you won't use all of it). Sprinkle with almonds, then the sugar-cinnamon mixture, gently pressing them into the dough.

5. Bake 20 to 25 minutes until lightly browned. Cool 10 minutes in pan on wire rack.

6. Bars are easier to cut while slightly warm. Lift from pan by ends of foil onto cutting board. Cut into 4 strips lengthwise, then 6 crosswise. Cut each bar diagonally in half to yield 2 triangles. Remove from foil to rack to cool completely.

PER BAR: 79 CAL • 1 G PRO • 8 G CAR • 0 G FIBER • 5 G FAT (3 G SAT FAT) • 19 MG CHOL • 15 MG SOD

Chewy Nut Bars

PLANNING TIP:
Refrigerate airtight with wax paper between layers up to 3 days.

CRUST
1 box (18.25 oz) devil's food cake mix
2½ sticks (1¼ cups) butter, melted
1 large egg
2 tsp vanilla extract

TOPPING
¾ cup light-brown sugar
3 large eggs
¼ cup light corn syrup
2 tsp vanilla extract
1 cup each (4 oz each) pecans, cashews and hazelnuts, coarsely chopped
1½ cups (9 oz) semisweet chocolate chips

1. Heat oven to 350°F. Line a 15 x 10-in. rimmed baking sheet with nonstick foil, letting foil extend above pan on both ends.
2. CRUST: Beat all ingredients in a large bowl with mixer on medium speed 1 minute or until blended. Spread evenly in pan.
3. Bake 15 minutes or until crust has risen and then fallen in center. Cool completely in pan on a wire rack.
4. TOPPING: Whisk brown sugar, eggs, corn syrup and vanilla in a medium bowl until smooth. Stir in nuts and chocolate chips. Spread evenly over crust.
5. Bake 35 minutes or until center no longer jiggles when pan is gently shaken. Cool 25 minutes in pan on a wire rack. Lift foil by ends and slide onto a cutting board. Cut lengthwise in 4 strips and crosswise in 8 to make 32 bars. Peel off foil.

PER BAR: 272 CAL • 3 G PRO • 27 G CAR • 2 G FIBER • 8 G FAT (7 G SAT FAT) • 47 MG CHOL • 212 MG SOD

Crispy Peanut Butter Bars

MAKES 60 / ACTIVE: 20 MIN
TOTAL: 1 HR 20 MIN (INCLUDES CHILLING TIME)

1 bag (10 oz) peanut butter chips
1 stick (½ cup) butter
6½ cups crisp rice cereal
1 bag (12 oz) semisweet chocolate chips
½ cup light corn syrup
½ cup honey-roasted peanuts, chopped

1. Line a 13 x 9-in. baking pan with nonstick foil to extend about 2 in. above narrow ends of pan.

2. Melt peanut butter chips and butter in a large bowl in microwave or in a heavy saucepan over low heat, stirring often, until thoroughly blended and smooth. Remove from heat, add cereal and stir until evenly coated.

3. Scrape into prepared pan, spread evenly, then cover with wax paper. Use another 13 x 9-in. pan or heavy book on top to press into an evenly compact layer, then remove wax paper. Place pan in freezer 10 minutes or until firm.

4. Melt chocolate chips as directed on bag. Add corn syrup and stir until well blended. Spread chocolate evenly on cereal mixture, then sprinkle with nuts. Top with wax paper and lightly press nuts into chocolate. Remove wax paper; refrigerate pan 1 hour or until firm.

5. Lift foil by ends onto cutting board. Cut crosswise in 10 strips, then cut each strip into 6 bars.
PER BAR: 89 CAL • 2 G PRO • 11 G CAR • 0 G FIBER • 5 G FAT (3 G SAT FAT) • 4 MG CHOL • 61 MG SOD

Triple Chocolate Cheesecake Bars

PLANNING TIP:
Refrigerate bars in an airtight container up to 3 days, or freeze up to 1 month (thaw 1 day in refrigerator before serving).

CRUST
24 Oreo cookies
3 Tbsp butter, melted

3 bricks (8 oz each) ⅓-less-fat cream cheese (Neufchâtel), softened
1 cup sugar
1 Tbsp cornstarch
3 large eggs, at room temperature
8 oz (scant 1 cup) reduced-fat sour cream
2 tsp vanilla extract
1 bar each (4 oz each) premium white, milk and semisweet baking chocolate

1. Heat oven to 300°F. Line a 9-in. square baking pan with foil, letting foil extend above pan on opposite sides. Coat with nonstick spray.
2. CRUST: Break cookies into food processor; pulse until fine crumbs form. Add butter; pulse to blend. Press firmly over bottom of pan. Freeze until firm.
3. Beat cream cheese, sugar and cornstarch in a large bowl with mixer on medium speed until smooth. On low speed, beat in eggs, 1 at a time, just until blended. Stir in sour cream and vanilla. Divide batter into 3 equal portions (about 1¾ cups each). Melt each flavor chocolate as inside of wrapper directs. Stir 1 flavor into each portion of batter. Spoon 2 Tbsp white chocolate batter into a ziptop bag, seal and set aside.
4. Pour milk chocolate batter over crust; spread evenly. Spoon on white chocolate batter; gently spread to cover milk chocolate layer. Repeat with semisweet batter. Cut tip off 1 corner of bag; pipe on white chocolate swirls.
5. Bake 45 minutes, or until center still jiggles slightly when shaken. Immediately transfer to a wire rack and refrigerate at least 3 hours.
6. Holding foil, lift cake to cutting board. Cut in 4 strips down, 8 across.

PER BAR: 199 CAL • 4 G PRO • 19 G CAR • 1 G FIBER • 12 G FAT (7 G SAT FAT) • 43 MG CHOL • 160 MG SOD

Margarita Cheesecake Bars

MAKES 42 / ACTIVE: 20 MIN
TOTAL: 50 MIN
(PLUS 3 HR CHILLING)

PLANNING TIP:
Can be made through Step 4 up to 1 day ahead. Garnish just before serving.

1 box (18.25 oz) lemon cake mix, prepared as box directs

⅓ cup fresh lime juice (grate lime zest first)
1 pkt (2½ tsp) unflavored gelatin
3 bricks (8 oz each) cream cheese, softened
½ cup sugar
1 Tbsp freshly grated lime zest
GARNISH: 1 lime

1. Heat oven to 350°F. Line a 13 x 9-in. baking pan with foil, letting foil extend about 2 in. above pan at both ends. Coat foil with nonstick spray.
2. Spread cake batter in prepared pan. Bake as box directs. Cool completely in pan on a wire rack. Holding foil ends, lift from pan. Trim rounded top (hump) off cake with a long serrated knife until flat. Holding foil ends, return cake to pan.
3. Pour lime juice into a small saucepan; sprinkle with gelatin. Let stand 1 minute, then stir over low heat 3 minutes until gelatin completely dissolves. Remove from heat.
4. Beat cream cheese, sugar and lime zest in a large bowl with mixer on medium speed 2 minutes or until fluffy. Slowly beat in gelatin mixture. Beat 1 minute to blend. Scrape onto cake, then spread evenly to edges. Refrigerate 1 hour to set, then cover loosely and refrigerate 2 hours or overnight.
5. TO SERVE: Lift from pan. Cut in 42 bars (dip knife in hot water; wipe clean between cuts). To garnish: With citrus zester, cut thin strips of zest off lime. Cut lime in quarters lengthwise, then crosswise in 11 slices. Top bars with lime and zest.

PER BAR: 139 CAL • 2 G PRO • 13 G CAR • 0 G FIBER • 9 G FAT (4 G SAT FAT) • 33 MG CHOL • 133 MG SOD

cakes, pies & tarts

Caribbean Ice Cream Pie

1 prepared reduced-fat graham cracker
   crust (6 oz)
2 pts light pineapple-coconut ice cream,
   slightly softened
1½ cups passion fruit sorbet
¼ cup orange or pineapple juice
3 Tbsp sugar
2 cups (1 lb) ripe red-fleshed papaya,
   peeled, seeded and diced
1½ cups diced fresh pineapple
2 kiwis, peeled, quartered lengthwise
   and sliced

1. Place crust (still in foil pan) into a 9-in. metal pie pan or on a small baking sheet. Spoon 1 pint of the ice cream into crust. Using back of spoon, gently press into an even layer. Freeze 1 hour or until firm.

2. Spread sorbet over ice cream into an even layer; freeze 1 hour.

3. Top sorbet layer with remaining ice cream, slightly mounding it in the center. Freeze pie 3 hours or until firm.

4. To serve, carefully lift the frozen pie from the foil pie plate and place on a serving plate. In a large bowl, combine juice and sugar; add fruit and toss. Spoon some of the fruit over top of pie. Cut into wedges and serve with remaining fruit.

TIP: Placing the prepared crust into a metal pie pan supports it while you pack it with ice cream and also helps it to chill faster.

PER SERVING: 278 CAL • 4 G PRO • 53 G CAR • 1 G FIBER • 5 G FAT (2 G SAT FAT) • 30 MG CHOL • 120 MG SOD

Tropical Cream Tart

SERVES 12 / ACTIVE: 15 MIN
TOTAL: 15 MIN (PLUS 3 HR CHILLING)

PLANNING TIP:
The crust can be made a day ahead and refrigerated. Make and add the filling up to 8 hours before serving.

CRUST
26 gingersnap cookies
½ stick (¼ cup) butter, melted

2 containers (6 oz each) pineapple fruit-on-the-bottom yogurt
1 tub (8 oz) frozen whipped topping, thawed
1 cup sweetened flaked coconut, chopped
GARNISH: chopped mango, pineapple and kiwi

1. Coat a 9-in. fluted tart pan with removable sides with nonstick spray.
2. CRUST: Break cookies into food processor; pulse until fine crumbs form. Add butter; pulse until blended. Press over bottom and up sides of tart pan. Refrigerate.
3. Stir yogurt in a large bowl to combine fruit. Fold in 2 cups whipped topping until blended, then the coconut. Spread in crust. Refrigerate 3 hours until set, or up to 8 hours.
4. Garnish just before serving.

PER SERVING: 211 CAL • 2 G PRO • 24 G CAR • 1 G FIBER • 12 G FAT (9 G SAT FAT) • 11 MG CHOL • 180 MG SOD

Lemon-Blueberry Chess Tart

SERVES 16 / ACTIVE: 20 MIN
TOTAL: 55 MIN (PLUS AT LEAST
4 HR CHILLING)

PLANNING TIP:
Can be prepared through Step 5 up to
2 days ahead. Cover once tart is chilled.

1 pkg (15 oz) refrigerated ready-to-use
pie crusts

FILLING

1½ cups sugar

2 Tbsp cornstarch

4 large eggs

½ stick (½ cup) unsalted butter, melted

¼ cup milk

1 Tbsp grated lemon zest

½ cup fresh lemon juice

¾ cup dried blueberries (see Note 1)

GARNISH: confectioners' sugar

1. Heat oven to 425°F. You'll need an 11 x 8-in. tart pan with removable sides and a baking sheet.
2. Unroll or unfold pie crusts. Fit to cover bottom and sides of tart pan. Brush overlapping edges with water; press to seal. Trim excess around edges. Prick bottom with a fork.
3. Line crust with foil; fill with ceramic pie weights, or dry beans or rice (see Note 2). Bake 5 minutes. Lift out foil and weights; bake 5 minutes more, or until just golden.
4. FILLING: Meanwhile, with a whisk, stir sugar and cornstarch in a large bowl to combine. Whisk in eggs, butter, milk and lemon zest and juice. Sprinkle crust with blueberries. Place pan with crust on baking sheet; slowly pour in Filling.
5. Place in oven, reduce temperature to 350°F and bake 25 minutes, or until filling sets. Cool completely in pan on a wire rack. Refrigerate at least 4 hours.
6. TO SERVE: Remove tart pan sides. Place 1-in.-wide foil strips diagonally across tart; dust with confectioners' sugar. Carefully lift strips; place diagonally across lines. Dust with confectioners' sugar; remove strips.

NOTE 1: Look for bags of dried blueberries in the produce or cereal section of your market. If unavailable, use dried cranberries.

NOTE 2: Ceramic pie weights, designed to prevent pastry shells from shrinking and puffing, are available in bakeware stores. Dried beans and rice serve the same purpose and can be reused endlessly.

PER SERVING: 221 CAL • 2 G PRO • 35 G CAR • 1 G FIBER • 8 G FAT (4 G SAT FAT) • 64 MG CHOL • 79 MG SOD

Ribbon Ice Cream Pie

SERVES 12 / ACTIVE: 25 MIN
TOTAL: 4½ HR (INCLUDES
FREEZING)

1 pint vanilla ice cream
1 ready-to-fill chocolate cookie crust
1 pint reduced-fat Dutch chocolate
    ice cream

1 pint strawberry ice cream
¼ cup fudge sauce
GARNISH: cut strawberries

1. Place vanilla ice cream in large bowl; stir until smooth but not melted. Spread into bottom of chocolate cookie crust. Freeze 30 minutes or until just firm.

2. Repeat as above with reduced-fat Dutch chocolate ice cream, then strawberry ice cream. Cover and freeze until firm. Before serving, slightly warm fudge sauce in microwave. Drizzle over pie; garnish with strawberries.

PER SERVING: 251 CAL • 4 G PRO • 32 G CAR • 1 G FIBER • 12 G FAT (5 G SAT FAT) • 22 MG CHOL • 124 MG SOD

Mini Peanut Butter Cheesecakes

MAKES 24 / ACTIVE: 20 MIN
TOTAL: 40 MIN (PLUS COOLING
AND AT LEAST 2 HR CHILLING)

PLANNING TIP:
Refrigerate with wax paper between layers up to 1 week, or freeze airtight up to 1 month (thaw in refrigerator).

1 pkg (9.5 oz) Keebler Fudge Shoppe
   Peanut Butter Filled cookies
2 bricks (8 oz each) ⅓-less-fat cream
   cheese (Neufchâtel), softened
1¼ cups sugar
1 cup creamy peanut butter
1 tsp vanilla extract
3 large eggs, at room temperature

CHOCOLATE GLAZE
3 oz semisweet baking chocolate
2 Tbsp each unsalted butter and light
   corn syrup
½ tsp vanilla extract

¼ cup roasted peanuts, chopped

1. Heat oven to 325°F. Line muffin pans with 24 paper (not foil) baking cups.
2. Break cookies into a food processor. Pulse until fine moist crumbs form. Press about 1 Tbsp evenly over bottom of each cup. Freeze until ready to fill.
3. Beat next 4 ingredients in a large bowl with mixer on medium speed until smooth. On low speed, beat in eggs, 1 at a time, just until blended. Spoon about 2½ Tbsp into each cup.
4. Bake 20 minutes, or until puffed. (Some may crack on top; that's OK.) Cool completely in pans on a wire rack.
5. Meanwhile, prepare Glaze: Microwave ingredients on medium, stirring until smooth. Cool slightly.
6. Peel off liners. Place cakes on a foil-lined baking sheet. Spoon glaze over tops; sprinkle with nuts. Refrigerate at least 2 hours for glaze to set.

PER CAKE: 258 CAL • 7 G PRO • 21 G CAR • 1 G FIBER • 17 G FAT (7 G SAT FAT) • 42 MG CHOL • 177 MG SOD

Chocolate-Speckled Angel Cake

SERVES 12 / ACTIVE: 30 MIN
TOTAL: 1½ HR

1. Prepare the Classic Angel Food Cake recipe, with these changes: After adding flour in Step 4, fold 2 oz finely chopped bittersweet chocolate and 1½ tsp grated orange zest into batter. Spread in prepared tube pan; bake as directed. Cool cake and remove from pan as directed.

2. To make Chocolate Glaze and serve: Place cake on a serving plate. In a 1-cup glass measure, combine 2 oz chopped bittersweet chocolate, 4 tsp butter and 2 tsp light corn syrup. Microwave on high 45 to 60 seconds until melted; whisk mixture until glaze is smooth. Let stand 10 minutes to thicken slightly, then spread over top of cake. Let stand 1 hour or until glaze sets. If desired, using photo as a guide, you can garnish the top of the cake with a 3.5-oz chocolate bar (we used Lindt's Intense Orange Dark Chocolate with Almond Slivers) cut into small triangles. Arrange chocolate pieces in glaze or serve alongside cake.

PER SERVING: 200 CAL • 5 G PRO • 37 G CAR • 1 G FIBER • 5 G FAT (3 G SAT FAT) • 3 MG CHOL • 106 MG SOD

Classic Angel Food Cake

SERVES 12 / ACTIVE: 20 MIN
TOTAL: 55 MIN

1 cup cake flour (not self-rising)
1¼ cups granulated sugar
¼ tsp salt
10 large egg whites (1⅓ to 1½ cups),
   at room temperature

1 tsp cream of tartar
2 tsp vanilla extract

1. Adjust oven rack to lowest position; heat oven to 350°F. You'll need a 10-in. tube pan with removable bottom. Line bottom with nonstick foil, cutting to fit around the tube; place back into pan.

2. Whisk together cake flour, ¼ cup sugar and the salt; transfer mixture to a sieve set over a small bowl.

3. In large bowl, beat the egg whites with electric mixer on medium speed 2 minutes or until frothy and well blended. Add the cream of tartar; increase speed to medium-high and beat until soft peaks start to form, about 3 minutes. While still beating, add the remaining 1 cup sugar in a slow stream; continue to beat until whites are very thick and hold firm peaks when beaters are lifted, about 3 minutes. Beat in the vanilla.

4. Transfer mixture to a large, wide bowl. Sift ⅓ of the flour mixture over whites; fold in with a rubber spatula. Repeat twice with the remaining flour, folding in until incorporated. Scrape batter into pan and spread evenly. Run a knife through the batter to remove any air pockets.

5. Bake 35 minutes, or until top of cake springs back when pressed with fingertip or a skewer inserted into cake comes out clean. Immediately invert the pan onto a wire rack. Cool completely, upside down.

6. To loosen cake, run a knife around all sides of pan. Lift cake out of pan by tube. Loosen cake from bottom; invert to unmold.

PER SERVING: 138 CAL • 4 G PRO • 30 G CAR • 0 G FIBER • 0 G FAT (0 G SAT FAT) • 0 MG CHOL • 95 MG SOD

Chocolate Cream Pie

SERVES 10 / ACTIVE: 30 MIN
TOTAL: 5 HR (INCLUDES CHILLING)

CRUST
10 whole chocolate graham crackers
2 Tbsp cold light butter
1 Tbsp lightly beaten egg white

FILLING
¼ cup each unsweetened Dutch process
   cocoa powder and cornstarch
2½ cups fat-free half-and-half
¾ cup sugar
2 oz unsweetened chocolate, melted
2 tsp light butter
1 tsp vanilla extract

TOPPING
1½ cups reduced-calorie whipped
   topping, thawed
GARNISH: chocolate curls (optional)

1. CRUST: Heat oven to 350°F. You'll need a 9-in. pie pan or plate coated with nonstick spray. Process graham crackers in food processor until finely ground. Add butter; pulse until coarse crumbs form. Add egg white; pulse until evenly moistened. Press crumb mixture evenly and firmly over bottom and sides of prepared pan. Bake 8 minutes; cool on wire rack.

2. FILLING: In bowl, whisk cocoa powder and cornstarch; whisk in 1½ cups of the half-and-half. In saucepan, heat remaining 1 cup half-and-half and the sugar over medium heat, stirring, until sugar is dissolved. Whisk in cocoa mixture and melted chocolate. Cook, stirring, until filling begins to bubble; continue to cook, whisking, until very thick, about 2 minutes longer. Off heat, whisk in butter and vanilla.

3. Spread filling in crust. Place plastic wrap onto surface of filling; refrigerate at least 4 hours. To serve, remove plastic wrap; spread whipped topping over filling and garnish with chocolate curls, if desired.

PER SERVING: 243 CAL • 4 G PRO • 42 G CAR • 2 G FIBER • 9 G FAT (5 G SAT FAT) • 7 MG CHOL • 211 MG SOD

Buttermilk Chocolate Swirl

2 cups all-purpose flour

1 cup sugar

1 tsp each baking powder and
  baking soda

½ tsp salt

¾ cup buttermilk

2 large eggs plus 1 large egg white

¼ cup canola oil

2 tsp vanilla extract

½ tsp almond extract or 2 tsp
  rum extract

4 oz bittersweet chocolate, broken up

GARNISH: confectioners' sugar

1. Heat oven to 350°F. You'll need an 8½ x 4½-in. loaf pan coated with nonstick spray. Line bottom and long sides of pan with wax paper; coat paper with nonstick spray.

2. Mix flour, sugar, baking powder, baking soda and salt in large bowl. Whisk buttermilk, eggs, egg white, oil and extracts in a medium bowl; stir into flour mixture until blended.

3. Melt chocolate in microwave on high about 1 minute, stirring every 15 seconds; stir in 1⅓ cups batter. Working quickly (chocolate batter will become firm and hard to swirl if you let it stand too long), pour some of the white batter over bottom of pan, then dollop with chocolate batter. Fill pan by alternating dollops of white and chocolate batter. Pull knife through batter to swirl.

4. Bake 1 hour or until pick inserted in center comes out clean. Cool in pan on wire rack 10 minutes. Remove from pan; put cake right side up on rack to cool. Dust with confectioners' sugar.

PER SERVING: 247 CAL • 5 G PRO • 38 G CAR • 1 G FIBER • 9 G FAT (3 G SAT FAT) • 36 MG CHOL • 267 MG SOD

Chocolate-Malt Ice Cream Cake

SERVES 16 / ACTIVE: 10 MIN
TOTAL: 10 MIN
(PLUS 4 HR FREEZING)

1 quart light vanilla ice cream,
    slightly softened
¼ cup malted milk powder

1 quart light chocolate ice cream
⅓ cup fat-free fudge topping
1 cup chopped malted milk balls

1. You'll need an 8-in. springform pan. In a large bowl, stir vanilla ice cream and malted milk powder until blended.
2. Spoon chocolate ice cream into bottom of pan; pack into a fairly even layer. Place spoonfuls of the fudge sauce over top. Sprinkle with ½ cup of the chopped malt balls.
3. Spread vanilla ice cream mixture over top. Freeze at least 4 hours or until firm.
4. TO SERVE: Remove sides of pan. Place on serving plate. Arrange remaining malt balls around edge.

PER SERVING: 204 CAL • 6 G PRO • 35 G CAR • 1 G FIBER • 4 G FAT (3 G SAT FAT) • 26 MG CHOL • 109 MG SOD

Mocha Marble Swirl Cheesecake

SERVES 16 / ACTIVE: 35 MIN
TOTAL: 2½ HR (PLUS 8 HR OF CHILLING AND 1 HR TO STAND AT ROOM TEMPERATURE)

1 (24-oz) container fat-free cottage cheese

CRUST
¾ cup cake flour (not self-rising)
2 Tbsp sugar
½ tsp grated lemon zest
2½ Tbsp cold light butter, cut into bits
1 Tbsp fat-free egg substitute

FILLING
2 bricks (8 oz each) ⅓-less-fat cream cheese (Neufchâtel), softened

¾ cup plus 2 Tbsp sugar
¼ cup cake flour (not self-rising)
½ cup fat-free sour cream, at room temperature
2 tsp vanilla extract
1 tsp grated lemon zest
¾ cup fat-free egg substitute, at room temperature
1½ Tbsp unsweetened cocoa powder, preferably Dutch process
2 tsp instant espresso powder

1. Place cottage cheese in a fine-mesh sieve set over a bowl; let stand 1 hour at room temperature to drain out excess liquid. Discard liquid.

2. Heat oven to 400°F. You'll need an 8-in. springform pan coated with nonstick spray; tightly cover outside of springform pan with double thickness of foil. You'll also need a large baking pan.

3. CRUST: Pulse flour, sugar and zest in food processor to combine. Add butter; pulse until mixture resembles coarse crumbs. Spoon egg substitute over crumbs; pulse until dough starts to clump. With floured hands, gather dough into a ball; press into even layer over bottom of springform pan. Bake 8 minutes or until set. Cool on wire rack. Reduce oven temperature to 350°F.

4. FILLING: Clean food processor; process cottage cheese until smooth. In a large bowl, beat cream cheese, ¾ cup sugar and the flour with an electric mixer on medium-high speed until light and fluffy. Beat in cottage cheese, sour cream, vanilla and lemon zest. With mixer on low, beat in egg substitute just until blended. Remove ½ cup filling to a small bowl; pour remaining filling over crust.

5. In a small cup, mix remaining 2 Tbsp sugar, the cocoa, espresso powder and 2 Tbsp hot water until blended and smooth; whisk into the reserved ½ cup filling. Spoon into a small ziptop bag, cut off a tip and pipe small puddles of the chocolate filling into white batter. Drag a skewer or knife through filling in spiral motions to create marbled effect.

6. Place cheesecake pan in larger baking pan and place on oven rack. Carefully pour enough hot water into larger pan to reach 1 in. up sides of springform pan. Bake 55 minutes or until cake jiggles slightly in the center.

7. Remove cake to a wire rack; carefully remove foil from pan. Using a thin-bladed knife, gently cut around top edge of cake where it meets pan. Place in refrigerator, uncovered; let chill at least 8 hours or overnight.

8. TO SERVE: Run a sharp knife around edge of pan to loosen cake; remove sides of pan. Let cheesecake stand at room temperature 1 hour before serving.

PER SERVING: 205 CAL • 10 G PRO • 24 G CAR • 0 G FIBER • 8 G FAT (5 G SAT FAT) • 26 MG CHOL • 308 MG SOD

Mocha Hazelnut Chiffon Cake

SERVES 24 / ACTIVE: 25 MIN
TOTAL: 1½ HR

2¼ cups cake flour
1¼ cups sugar
1 Tbsp baking powder
½ tsp salt
½ cup unsweetened cocoa powder
   (not Dutch process)
2 Tbsp espresso powder
½ cup boiling water
¼ cup cold water
⅓ cup canola oil
5 large egg yolks

10 large egg whites
2 Tbsp hazelnut liqueur (Frangelico)
1 tsp vanilla extract
1 tsp cream of tartar

CHOCOLATE GLAZE
4 oz semisweet chocolate, broken up
½ cup fat-free half-and-half
GARNISH: toasted chopped
   hazelnuts

1. Heat oven to 325°F. Place oven rack at position just below center. You'll need a 10-in. tube pan with removable bottom. Whisk flour, ¾ cup sugar, baking powder and salt in a large bowl.

2. Stir cocoa and espresso with boiling water in a medium bowl until dissolved; add cold water, oil, yolks, liqueur and vanilla. Stir cocoa mixture into flour mixture until blended.

3. Beat whites and cream of tartar in a large bowl with mixer on medium-high speed until soft peaks form when beaters are lifted. Gradually beat in remaining ½ cup sugar. Beat until glossy and stiff peaks form.

4. Stir ¼ of beaten whites into cocoa-flour batter to lighten. Gently fold batter into rest of whites until no white streaks remain. Pour into ungreased pan.

5. Bake 1 hour or until wooden skewer inserted into cake comes out clean. Invert pan onto neck of a tall, narrow bottle, such as a wine bottle; cool completely. Run a thin knife around sides of cake; remove pan sides. Repeat with bottom of cake. Invert onto cake plate. Remove pan.

6. GLAZE: Melt chocolate in microwave on high about 1 minute, stirring every 15 seconds. Whisk in half-and-half. Pour glaze over cake, spreading top with spatula. Sprinkle with hazelnuts.

PER SERVING: 157 CAL • 3 G PRO • 23 G CAR • 1 G FIBER • 6 G FAT (2 G SAT FAT) • 44 MG CHOL • 128 MG SOD

No-Bake Mocha Roll

PLANNING TIP:
You'll need a serving surface at least 14 x 4 in. If you don't have a platter or tray that size, cover a piece of heavy cardboard, a plastic-foam board or a baking sheet with foil. Can be made up to 2 days ahead.

1 purchased frozen poundcake (10.75 oz), brought to room temperature

CUSTARD
½ cup sugar
2 Tbsp cornstarch
2 large egg yolks
1⅓ cups whole milk
¼ cup instant coffee granules
1 cup (6 oz) semisweet chocolate chips
¾ cup heavy (whipping) cream
GARNISH: 14 chocolate-covered coffee beans

1. Using a long knife, trim crust off poundcake so cake resembles a brick (you won't need the crust). Cut cake lengthwise into 6 equal slices. Place slices, long sides touching, side by side on a sheet of wax paper on work surface. Top with wax paper.

2. With a rolling pin, roll slices into a rectangle, roughly 12½ x 9½ in. (slices should fuse together). If cake cracks, patch with crumbs (from ends) while rolling. Slide, still between wax paper, onto a flat baking sheet; set aside.

3. CUSTARD: Whisk sugar and cornstarch in a medium saucepan until blended. Whisk yolks in a small bowl to blend. Whisk milk into sugar mixture and, stirring occasionally, bring to a boil. Boil, stirring constantly, 1 minute. Remove from heat; gradually whisk about half into the yolks. Pour yolk mixture back into saucepan and stir gently over medium heat until a few bubbles break through the surface. Cook, stirring, 2 minutes (to cook yolks).

4. Remove from heat. Add instant coffee and chocolate chips; stir until coffee dissolves and chips melt. Remove ½ cup and reserve.

5. Remove wax paper from top of cake. Spread remaining custard evenly to about ¼ in. from edges. Cover surface of reserved custard in bowl and on cake directly with wax paper (to keep a skin from forming). Refrigerate both 20 minutes until cooled.

6. Beat cream in a medium bowl with mixer on medium-high speed until stiff peaks form when beaters are lifted. Fold in reserved ½ cup custard and refrigerate.

7. Have serving surface ready (see Planning Tip). Carefully lift wax paper off custard. Using wax paper under cake as an aid, roll up cake from a long side, jelly roll–style. Gently roll onto serving platter.

8. Scrape ⅓ cup of the reserved whipped cream mixture into a qt-size ziptop bag; seal and set aside. Use rest to frost cake. Snip tip off corner of bag and pipe 14 large dots down length of cake. Place a chocolate-covered coffee bean on each. Lightly cover cake with plastic wrap and refrigerate at least 2 hours until frosting is firm, or cover loosely and refrigerate up to 2 days.

PER SERVING: 258 CAL • 3 G PRO • 30 G CAR • 0 G FIBER • 15 G FAT (8 G SAT FAT) • 76 MG CHOL • 100 MG SOD

Peaches & Cream Chiffon Cake

SERVES 12 / ACTIVE: 35 MIN
TOTAL: 1 HR

CAKE

5 large egg whites
4 large egg yolks
¼ tsp cream of tartar
¾ cup granulated sugar
¼ cup peach nectar
1 Tbsp canola oil
1 vanilla bean, split, seeds scraped, or
   1 Tbsp vanilla extract
¼ tsp salt
1 cup cake flour (not self-rising)

FILLING AND CREAM

4 cups (2 lb) ripe peaches,
   pitted and sliced
1½ Tbsp lemon juice
¼ cup granulated sugar
2 Tbsp confectioners' sugar
1 cup nonfat Greek yogurt
½ cup heavy cream

1. Heat oven to 325°F. Coat an 8 x 3-in. springform pan with nonstick spray.
2. CAKE: Beat egg whites and cream of tartar in large bowl with mixer at medium speed until soft peaks form when beaters are lifted. Gradually beat in ¼ cup of the sugar; beat on high until stiff yet billowy peaks form. In a medium bowl, beat the egg yolks, remaining ½ cup sugar, peach nectar, oil, vanilla bean and salt on medium-high until light in color and slightly thickened, about 5 minutes.
3. Pour half of the yolk mixture over whites and sift half of the flour on top; fold until just blended. Fold in remaining yolk mixture and flour. Scrape batter into prepared pan. Bake 34 to 36 minutes, until cake rises slightly above top edge of pan, is golden brown and a pick inserted in center comes out clean. Remove from oven; cool cake on a wire rack 3 minutes. Invert cake onto wire rack, remove pan, reinvert and cool completely.
4. FILLING AND CREAM: Toss peaches, lemon juice and granulated sugar in a medium bowl. Let stand while cake bakes. Stir confectioners' sugar into yogurt in a medium bowl. In a small bowl, beat cream until stiff peaks form; fold into yogurt mixture and refrigerate.
5. Trim the top of the cake, then split into 2 layers. Place bottom layer on plate; spoon half the peaches with juices over top, then spread half of the cream. Top with remaining cake layer, peaches and a dollop of cream. Serve remaining cream on the side.

PER SERVING: 218 CAL • 6 G PRO • 34 G CAR • 1 G FIBER • 7 G FAT (3 G SAT FAT) • 83 MG CHOL • 85 MG SOD

Cinnamon Pecan Streusel Cake

SERVES 24 / ACTIVE: 25 MIN
TOTAL: 1 HR

STREUSEL

¼ cup packed dark brown sugar
⅓ cup uncooked quick-cooking oats
2 Tbsp all-purpose flour
¼ tsp ground cinnamon
1 Tbsp light stick butter (we used
   Land O'Lakes Light), softened
2 tsp water
½ cup coarsely chopped pecans

CAKE

1¾ cups granulated sugar
1½ sticks (¾ cup) light butter (we
   used Land O'Lakes Light), softened
2 tsp ground cinnamon
½ tsp ground allspice
1 tsp vanilla extract
¾ tsp baking soda
⅛ tsp salt
3 large eggs
1½ cups each all-purpose flour and
   whole-wheat flour
1 container (8 oz) reduced-fat sour cream

1. STREUSEL: Mix brown sugar, oats, flour and cinnamon in small bowl. Add butter and water; rub between fingers until evenly moistened. Stir in pecans; press together to form small clumps.

2. CAKE: Heat oven to 350°F. Line a 13 x 9 x 2-in. baking pan with nonstick foil, letting ends of foil extend about 2 in. above pan on short sides.

3. Beat sugar, butter, spices, vanilla, baking soda and salt in large bowl with mixer 3 minutes until blended. Beat in eggs, 1 at a time, beating well after each. Alternately beat in flours with sour cream on low speed until just blended.

4. Spread batter evenly in pan, sprinkle with streusel and bake 35 minutes or until a wooden pick inserted in center comes out clean. Cool completely in pan on a wire rack. Lift cake by foil ends onto cutting board. Cut into 24 squares.

PER SERVING: 189 CAL • 3 G PRO • 30 G CAR • 2 G FIBER • 7 G FAT (3 G SAT FAT) • 38 MG CHOL • 119 MG SOD

Ice Cream "Cupcakes"

MAKES 4 / ACTIVE: 30 MIN
TOTAL: 30 MIN (PLUS AT LEAST
1 HR FREEZING)

PLANNING TIP:
Can be frozen 1 week.

½ cup milk-chocolate chips
1 pint ice cream, any flavor
⅔ cup frozen whipped topping, thawed
Liquid food colors (optional)
GARNISH: 4 Keebler Bug Bites
    cinnamon graham crackers,
    decorated (directions follow)

1. Using 32 foil baking cups with paper liners, assemble 4 stacks (8 cups in each), with a foil cup on top.

2. Melt chocolate as package directs. Brush inside of the top foil cups with chocolate. Freeze until set.

3. Drop 1 scoop ice cream into each chocolate cup; remove from stack of cups and return to freezer.

4. If tinting topping, divide between cups and tint pastel colors. Spoon into ziptop bags, cut a corner off each and pipe topping on ice cream. Decorate with a cookie.

TO DECORATE COOKIES: Mix ½ cup confectioners' sugar and 2 tsp water until smooth. Divide among 5 cups (about 2 tsp each). Leave 1 white; tint others with food color. Spoon each into a small ziptop bag; snip a tiny tip off 1 corner. Pipe features; let dry.

PER CUPCAKE: 286 CAL • 2 G PRO • 33 G CAR • 0 G FIBER • 16 G FAT (11 G SAT FAT) • 29 MG CHOL • 63 MG SOD

Creamsicle Cupcakes

MAKES 24 / ACTIVE: 20 MIN
TOTAL: 45 MIN

PLANNING TIP:
Unfrosted cupcakes can be stored covered at room temperature up to 3 days or frozen airtight up to 1 month. Thaw before frosting. Frosted cupcakes can be refrigerated up to 1 day.

Basic Batter (see recipe on page 16)
½ cup orange juice
2 tsp grated orange zest

CREAMSICLE FROSTING
1½ cups heavy (whipping) cream
½ cup confectioners' sugar
1 Tbsp grated orange zest
Liquid orange food color (optional)
GARNISH: thin strips orange zest

1. Heat oven to 350°F. Line 24 regular-size (2½-in.-diameter) muffin cups with paper or foil liners.
2. Prepare Basic Batter, using only ½ cup milk and adding orange juice and zest. Spoon evenly in muffin cups.
3. Bake 22 to 25 minutes until a wooden pick inserted in center of cupcakes comes out clean and tops are golden. Cool in pans on a wire rack 5 minutes before removing from pans to rack to cool completely.
4. FROSTING: Beat first 3 ingredients in medium bowl on medium-high speed until soft peaks form when beaters are lifted. Tint with food color; beat just until blended. Frost and garnish cupcakes.

PER CUPCAKE: 225 CAL • 3 G PRO • 26 G CAR • 0 G FIBER • 13 G FAT (7 G SAT FAT) • 73 MG CHOL • 64 MG SOD

Peach Melba Cupcakes

MAKES 12 / ACTIVE: 20 MIN
TOTAL: 1 HR

1. Prepare the Classic Angel Food Cake recipe on page 31, with these changes: You'll need 24 jumbo paper cupcake liners. Double up the liners, 2 per cupcake, and arrange on a large baking sheet. After adding flour in Step 4, spoon the batter into a gallon-size ziptop bag; seal bag and cut off a ½-in. corner. Pipe the batter into the liners, filling each almost to the top. Smooth tops with an offset spatula. Bake 20 minutes, or until pick inserted in centers comes out clean. Cool on baking sheet on wire rack.

2. MELBA SAUCE: Purée in a blender a thawed 10-oz package frozen raspberries in syrup. Scrape berry mixture through a fine-mesh sieve set over a medium bowl to remove seeds; discard seeds.

3. TO ASSEMBLE CUPCAKES: You'll need a thawed 1-lb bag frozen sliced peaches (any thick slices should be cut into thinner slices). If desired, toss peaches with ¼ cup sugar. Carefully peel back inner paper liner; remove cupcake. Slice off rounded top with a serrated knife; cut top into quarters. Place cupcake bottom back into outer paper liner and spoon some Melba Sauce over cut surface. Top with a dollop of whipped topping. Place 3 or 4 peach slices into whipped topping. Drizzle with more sauce; add another dollop of whipped topping. Stick cupcake-top quarters into cream.

PER CUPCAKE: 229 CAL • 4 G PRO • 44 G CAR • 2 G FIBER • 3 G FAT (3 G SAT FAT) • 0 MG CHOL • 95 MG SOD

Pear-Ginger Bundt Cake

SERVES 24 / ACTIVE: 25 MIN
TOTAL: 1½ HR

¾ cup water

2¼ cups sugar

1 2-in. piece fresh ginger, peeled
and sliced

3 cups all-purpose flour

2½ tsp baking powder

½ tsp salt

1 cup milk

⅔ cup light olive oil or canola oil

3 large eggs plus 1 large egg white

1 tsp vanilla extract

1 medium Bosc pear, peeled, cored
and chopped (1 cup)

3 Tbsp minced crystallized ginger

2 tsp turbinado sugar (such as
Sugar in the Raw)

GARNISH: strips of crystallized ginger

1. Heat oven to 350°F. You'll need a nonstick 12- to 15-cup-capacity Bundt pan coated with nonstick spray. Bring water, ¾ cup sugar and the sliced ginger to boil in a small saucepan. Reduce heat to low; simmer, uncovered, 15 minutes or until syrupy. Discard ginger slices.

2. Meanwhile, mix flour, remaining 1½ cups sugar, the baking powder and salt in a large bowl.

3. Whisk together milk, olive oil, ½ cup cooled ginger syrup, the eggs, egg white and vanilla in a medium bowl. Stir into flour mixture until just blended.

4. Stir chopped pear and crystallized ginger into batter. Pour into pan; bake 50 minutes or until wooden skewer inserted into cake comes out clean. Cool in pan on a wire rack 15 minutes before inverting. Brush hot cake with remaining ginger syrup, sprinkle with turbinado sugar and let cool. Top with strips of crystallized ginger, if desired.

PER SERVING: 205 CAL • 3 G PRO • 33 G CAR • 1 G FIBER • 7 G FAT (1 G SAT FAT) • 28 MG CHOL • 105 MG SOD

Strawberry Cannoli

MAKES 12 / ACTIVE: 20 MIN
TOTAL: 20 MIN (PLUS OVERNIGHT
DRAINING)

The sugar cones replace the usual pastry shells, which can be hard to make or find in stores.

PLANNING TIP:
Prepare through Step 3 at least 24 hours, or up to 2 days, ahead. Fill cones just before serving.

1 pint (12 oz) strawberries, rinsed,
   hulled and halved
2 Tbsp granulated sugar
1 tub (15 oz) whole-milk ricotta cheese
4 oz cream cheese
1 cup confectioners' sugar
1 box (4 or 5¼ oz) sugar cones
   (12 cones)
¼ tsp almond extract
GARNISH: mini–chocolate chips and
   sliced strawberries

1. At least 1 day before serving, proceed through Step 3. Line a colander and a medium-size strainer with a sturdy paper towel; set each in a bowl.
2. Pulse strawberries and granulated sugar in food processor until coarsely chopped. Scrape into colander, top with a paper towel and refrigerate overnight to drain well (this is important). Clean processor.
3. Put ricotta, cream cheese and confectioners' sugar in processor; pulse until smooth. Transfer to strainer, cover with a paper towel and refrigerate overnight.
4. Just before serving: Prop cones upright in tall glasses partially filled with granulated sugar to support cones. Fold drained berries and almond extract into ricotta mixture. Spoon into a gallon-size ziptop bag. Cut ½ in. off a corner; pipe filling into cones and garnish.

PER SERVING: 188 CAL • 6 G PRO • 24 G CAR • 1 G FIBER • 8 G FAT (5 G SAT FAT) • 28 MG CHOL • 93 MG SOD

Lime & Berry Loaf Cake

SERVES 16 / ACTIVE: 15 MIN
TOTAL: 7 HR (INCLUDES CHILLING)

PLANNING TIP:
Can be made through Step 5 up to
3 days ahead.

1 can (6 oz) frozen limeade, thawed
½ cup sugar
14 imported Italian savoiardi
   ladyfingers (see Note)

2 tsp unflavored gelatin
1 tub (8 oz) frozen creamy whipped
   topping, thawed
1½ pint (18 oz) fresh raspberries
1½ pint (18 oz) fresh blackberries

1. Rinse a 9 x 5-in. loaf pan (about 8-cup capacity). Line pan with plastic wrap, letting some extend above sides. Wrap a piece of thin cardboard, cut to fit bottom of pan, with foil. Place in pan for easy unmolding.

2. Pour limeade into a clear 2-cup measure; add cold water to equal 2 cups. Stir in sugar until dissolved. Pour ⅔ cup into a shallow medium bowl.

3. Dip both sides of each ladyfinger into bowl. Use 7 to cover bottom of pan. Reserve remaining on plastic wrap.

4. Sprinkle gelatin over ¼ cup limeade mixture in a small saucepan; let stand 1 to 2 minutes to soften. Stir over low heat until gelatin granules completely dissolve. Pour into a medium bowl, add remaining limeade mixture and refrigerate, stirring occasionally, 30 minutes or until consistency of unbeaten egg whites. Add a large spoonful whipped topping; whisk until blended. Whisk in remaining topping.

5. Scatter about ½ the berries over the ladyfingers in pan. Spread with ½ the limeade cream. Place reserved ladyfingers crosswise down middle of loaf. Spread with remaining cream; top with rest of berries. Refrigerate at least 6 hours or until set.

6. TO SERVE: Lift plastic wrap by sides onto serving plate. Peel plastic wrap down sides; cut or slide plastic wrap away from loaf. Leave on cardboard to slice.

NOTE: Italian savoiardi ladyfingers are crisp and are often longer than the soft sponge cake–like variety.

PER SERVING: 159 CAL • 1 G PRO • 31 G CAR • 3 G FIBER • 3 G FAT (3 G SAT FAT) • 1 MG CHOL • 21 MG SOD

Pear-Raspberry Jelly Roll Shortcakes

SERVES 10 / ACTIVE: 30 MIN
TOTAL: 1½ HR
(INCLUDES COOLING)

TOPPING

2 ripe red-skinned pears, cored and
   thinly sliced
¼ cup sugar
½ pint fresh raspberries

JELLY ROLL

1 Tbsp plus ½ cup cake flour (not
   self-rising)
½ tsp baking powder

5 large egg whites, at room
   temperature
¾ cup granulated sugar
½ cup fat-free egg substitute
1 tsp vanilla extract
2 Tbsp minced crystallized ginger
Confectioners' sugar, for dusting
½ cup reduced-calorie raspberry
   preserves
1⅓ cups reduced-calorie whipped
   topping, thawed

1. TOPPING: Toss pears and sugar in a bowl; stir in raspberries. Refrigerate.

2. JELLY ROLL: Heat oven to 400°F. You'll need a 15½ x 10½ x 1-in. jelly roll pan coated with nonstick spray; line with wax paper. Coat paper with nonstick spray; dust with 1 Tbsp cake flour. In small bowl, whisk remaining ½ cup flour and baking powder.

3. In large bowl with mixer on medium-high speed, beat egg whites until soft peaks start to form. Gradually beat in ½ cup of the granulated sugar. At high speed, continue to beat whites until stiff yet billowy peaks form.

4. In a medium bowl, beat egg substitute with remaining ¼ cup granulated sugar 3 minutes, or until lightened in color. Add vanilla. At low speed, beat in half of the flour mixture; fold into egg whites with remaining flour mixture and ginger. Spread in prepared pan. Bake 12 minutes, or until top springs back when pressed. Let cool on rack 2 minutes.

5. Dust a clean kitchen towel with confectioners' sugar. Loosen cake from sides of pan; invert cake onto towel. Remove pan; peel off paper. Starting from a short end, roll up cake in towel; place seam-side down on rack and cool completely, about 30 minutes.

6. Scrape preserves through mesh sieve to remove seeds. Unroll cake; spread with preserves. Reroll cake; place seam-side down on cutting board. Trim ends of cake roll.

7. To serve, place a ½-inch slice jelly roll on a plate. Top with ¼ cup fruit and 2 Tbsp whipped topping. Lean another slice against stack. Dust with confectioners' sugar.

PER SERVING: 191 CAL • 4 G PRO • 44 G CAR • 2 G FIBER • 1 G FAT (1 G SAT FAT) • 0 MG CHOL • 81 MG SOD

Strawberry-Peach Butterflies

MAKES 12 / ACTIVE: 30 MIN
TOTAL: 4 HR (INCLUDES CHILLING)

PLANNING TIP:
Can be made through Step 5 up to
2 days ahead.

1 purchased frozen poundcake
(10.75 oz), thawed

1 box (3 oz) peach gelatin
1 cup heavy (whipping) cream
1½ cups strawberries, hulled, cut
lengthwise in wedges
1 cup diced, peeled peach
1 Tbsp sugar

1. You'll need a 2¼-in. round metal cookie cutter and a pastry bag fitted with a large star tip. Line 12 regular muffin cups with foil liners.
2. Using cookie cutter, cut 4 circles from top through to bottom of cake. Cut each log into 6 rounds. Put 1 in bottom of each lined cup; set aside remaining 12.
3. Add ¾ cup boiling water to gelatin in a medium bowl. Stir until dissolved. Refrigerate, stirring occasionally, 15 minutes or until consistency of unbeaten egg whites.
4. Beat ½ cup cream in a medium bowl with mixer on medium-high speed until soft peaks form when beaters are lifted. Stir a large spoonful into peach mixture, then fold in rest of cream. Fold in strawberries and peach.
5. Immediately spoon into lined cups; top with reserved poundcake rounds. Cover pan tightly with plastic wrap; refrigerate at least 3 hours or until "cakes" are firm.
6. TO SERVE: Remove liners; cut cakes in half. Place 2 halves, round sides touching (see photo, above) on plates.
7. Beat rest of cream and the sugar in a small bowl with mixer until stiff peaks form when beaters are lifted. Spoon into pastry bag; pipe line down center.

PER SERVING: 191 CAL • 2 G PRO • 20 G CAR • 1 G FIBER • 11 G FAT (7 G SAT FAT) • 48 MG CHOL • 95 MG SOD

Frozen Berry
Angel Shortcake

SERVES 12 / ACTIVE: 30 MIN
TOTAL: 5 HR (INCLUDES FREEZING)

1. Prepare the Classic Angel Food Cake recipe on page 31, with these changes: Line the bottom of a 9 x 3-in. springform pan with nonstick foil, then attach the sides of the pan. Substitute raspberry extract for the vanilla in Step 3, and add 3 drops liquid red food color with the extract. Spread in prepared pan and bake as directed. Cool the cake completely, in pan, upside down on a wire rack. To loosen cake, run a thin-bladed knife around sides of pan; remove pan sides. Invert cake and remove pan bottom.

2. To assemble Shortcake: Using a serrated knife, cut cake into 2 layers. Place bottom layer, cut side up, on pan bottom and spread with ⅓ cup strawberry topping. Spoon 3 cups slightly softened lowfat strawberry ice cream or frozen yogurt over topping. Spread another ⅓ cup strawberry topping over ice cream. Top with remaining cake layer, cut side down. Freeze at least 4 hours or overnight. (Once the cake is frozen, it can be wrapped and stored in freezer up to 2 weeks.)

3. TO SERVE: Transfer frozen cake to a serving plate. Frost with 2 cups thawed reduced-calorie whipped topping or lightly sweetened whipped cream. Decorate with strawberries or raspberries. Refrigerate 30 minutes to soften slightly before serving.

PER SERVING: 268 CAL • 5 G PRO • 57 G CAR • 1 G FIBER • 2 G FAT (2 G SAT FAT) • 0 MG CHOL • 116 MG SOD

Lemon-Ricotta Bundles with Blueberry Sauce

SERVES 6 / ACTIVE: 40 MIN
TOTAL: 6 HR (INCLUDES
DRAINING RICOTTA)

LEMON-RICOTTA FILLING

1 container (15 oz) part-skim ricotta
3 Tbsp confectioners' sugar
½ tsp grated lemon zest
1 Tbsp lemon juice
½ tsp vanilla extract

CRÊPES

2 large eggs
1 cup nonfat milk
½ cup all-purpose flour
2 Tbsp light stick butter, melted
2 Tbsp granulated sugar
1 tsp vanilla extract

BLUEBERRY SAUCE

3 cups fresh blueberries
⅓ cup granulated sugar
2 Tbsp lemon juice
¼ tsp ground cinnamon
¼ tsp grated lemon zest

1 roll green apple–flavor Fruit by the
   Foot fruit leather
GARNISH: confectioners' sugar
   (optional)

PLANNING TIP: You can make filling, crêpes and sauce up to 2 days ahead and refrigerate. Bring crêpes and sauce to room temperature before assembling.

1. FILLING: Mix ingredients in medium bowl until blended. Scrape into a sieve set over a bowl, cover and refrigerate 4 to 6 hours, until excess liquid drains from ricotta.

2. Meanwhile, make crêpe batter: Combine ingredients in a blender; process until smooth. Cover; let rest in refrigerator about 1 hour. You'll need sixteen 7-in. squares of wax paper.

3. CRÊPES: Lightly coat a 6-in. nonstick skillet (measure pan across bottom) with nonstick spray. Place skillet over medium-low heat until pan is hot. Add 2 Tbsp batter, tilt skillet and gently swirl until batter covers bottom. Cook 1 minute, or until underside of crêpe is lightly browned. Loosen edges with a spatula and flip crêpe over. Cook other side 30 seconds. Slide crêpe onto a square of wax paper. Repeat with remaining batter, lightly spraying skillet each time and stacking cooked crêpes between wax paper (the recipe makes 16 crêpes; you'll need only 12).

4. BLUEBERRY SAUCE: Bring 2 cups of the blueberries and remaining sauce ingredients except lemon zest to a boil in a medium saucepan over medium-high heat. Cook 3 minutes, or until berries soften and release their juices. Transfer mixture to a blender and purée; scrape through a fine-mesh sieve to remove seeds. Stir in lemon zest and reserve.

5. TO ASSEMBLE: Discard drained liquid from filling. Unroll fruit leather and cut twelve 8-in.-long, ¼-in.-wide strips. Place a rounded Tbsp ricotta filling in center of a crêpe. Gather up edges to form a small bundle and tie with a strip of fruit leather (see photo). Make 11 more bundles.

6. TO SERVE: Place 2 bundles on each plate. Spoon ¼ cup sauce around bundles and sprinkle with some of the remaining blueberries. Dust with confectioners' sugar, if desired. Serve immediately.

PER SERVING: 294 CAL • 12 G PRO • 42 G CAR • 2 G FIBER • 9 G FAT (5 G SAT FAT) • 80 MG CHOL • 149 MG SOD

Berry-Cheese Braid

SERVES 8 / ACTIVE: 5 MIN
TOTAL: 30 MIN

1 tub (8 oz) strawberry cream cheese,
   at room temperature
1 large egg, yolk and white separated
¼ cup plus 1 Tbsp sugar
1 sheet frozen puff pastry (from a
   17.3-oz box), thawed

1. Heat oven to 400°F. You'll need a baking sheet.
2. Stir cream cheese, egg yolk and ¼ cup sugar until blended. Slightly beat egg white in a small bowl.
3. Place puff pastry lengthwise in center of baking sheet and unfold. With a rolling pin, roll out to a 12-in.-long rectangle. Spoon cheese filling in 2½-in.-wide strip down center.
4. On both sides of filling, cut 1-in.-wide strips from filling to edge. Fold strips at an angle across filling, overlapping and alternating from side to side. Brush with egg white; sprinkle with remaining Tbsp sugar.
5. Bake 25 minutes until puffed and golden. Cool slightly on sheet on a wire rack. Serve warm or at room temperature.

DIFFERENT TAKES

- Add chocolate chips to filling.
- Scatter sliced almonds on top before sprinkling with sugar.
- Use Brown Sugar N' Cinnamon Spice Swirls Cream Cheese Spread instead of the strawberry cream cheese.

PER SERVING: 300 CAL • 4 G PRO • 27 G CAR • 1 G FIBER • 20 G FAT (6 G SAT FAT) • 55 MG CHOL • 194 MG SOD

Chocolate-Raspberry Turnovers

SERVES 6 / ACTIVE: 30 MIN
TOTAL: 42 MIN

12 sheets fillo dough (each about
   14 x 9 in.), thawed if frozen

1 bar (3.5 oz) Lindt Lindor truffles
   (18 pieces)
½ pint fresh raspberries

1. Heat oven to 375°F. You'll need a baking sheet. Unfold fillo; cover with plastic wrap to prevent drying.
2. To make each turnover: Remove 1 sheet fillo; lightly coat with nonstick spray or brush with melted butter. Fold in thirds lengthwise; lightly spray or brush top. Place 1 piece chocolate about ½ in. from bottom end of strip; top with 1 raspberry. Fold lower right corner over filling, forming a triangle. Continue folding triangles to other end of strip. Place on baking sheet. Repeat to make 12.
3. Bake 10 to 12 minutes until golden. Remove to a wire rack to cool. Melt remaining 6 pieces chocolate in microwave; drizzle over turnovers. Serve warm or at room temperature. Garnish with remaining raspberries.

PER 2 TURNOVERS: 175 CAL • 3 G PRO • 21 G CAR • 1 G FIBER • 10 G FAT (6 G SAT FAT) • 2 MG CHOL • 121 MG SOD

Pumpkin Spice Muffins

MAKES 20 / ACTIVE: 20 MIN
TOTAL: 1 HR

½ cup each granulated sugar and packed
   light-brown sugar
6 Tbsp unsalted butter, softened
2 tsp each ground cinnamon and vanilla
   extract
1½ tsp ground ginger
½ tsp ground cloves
1 tsp each baking powder and baking soda
¾ tsp salt
2 large eggs plus 2 large egg whites
1¼ cups pumpkin purée
2½ cups all-purpose flour
½ cup milk
1½ cups fresh or frozen cranberries,
   halved

MAPLE DRIZZLE
⅔ cup confectioners' sugar
3 Tbsp pure maple syrup
GARNISH: toasted pumpkin seeds

1. Heat oven to 350°F. You'll need 20 muffin cups lined with paper liners. Beat sugars, butter, spices, vanilla, baking powder, baking soda and salt in a large bowl with mixer on medium speed 2 minutes or until blended.

2. Beat in eggs and whites. Beat in pumpkin purée on low speed until just combined. Alternately beat in flour, then milk, until just blended. Stir in berries.

3. Put ¼ cup batter in each muffin cup. Bake 30 minutes or until toothpick inserted into centers comes out clean. Cool 5 minutes in pans on rack, remove from pans and cool completely.

4. DRIZZLE: Up to 4 hours before serving, stir ingredients in small bowl until smooth. Scrape into a small ziptop bag. Cut a small tip from one corner of bag and drizzle over cupcakes. Garnish with pumpkin seeds.

PER SERVING: 177 CAL • 3 G PRO • 31 G CAR • 1 G FIBER • 5 G FAT (3 G SAT FAT) • 32 MG CHOL • 189 MG SOD

Lemon Angel Torte

SERVES 8 / ACTIVE: 30 MIN
TOTAL: 2½ HR (INCLUDES CHILLING)

LEMON FILLING
¾ tsp unflavored gelatin
1 Tbsp water
½ cup granulated sugar
2 Tbsp cornstarch
½ tsp grated lemon zest
¼ cup lemon juice
⅓ cup each orange juice and water
¼ cup reduced-fat sour cream
½ cup sliced almonds, toasted
Confectioners' sugar, for dusting

1. CAKE: Line a 9 x 5 x 3-in. loaf pan with double thickness of nonstick foil, letting foil extend 2 in. over ends of pan. Prepare ½ of the Classic Angel Food Cake batter on page 31, adding 1 tsp almond extract and ½ tsp grated lemon zest instead of the vanilla extract in Step 3.

2. Bake 28 minutes, or until a skewer inserted into center comes out clean. Immediately invert the pan onto a wire rack. Cool completely. To loosen cake, run a knife around long sides of pan. Lift out of pan by foil ends and place in freezer covered with foil to firm up.

3. LEMON FILLING: Sprinkle gelatin over water in small cup to soften. In medium saucepan, whisk sugar and cornstarch until blended. Stir in lemon zest and juice, orange juice and water. Cook over medium heat, stirring constantly, until mixture comes to a gentle boil. Stir in gelatin. Boil 1 minute, stirring constantly, until it thickens. Transfer to a bowl; stir in sour cream. Cover surface of filling with plastic wrap; let cool to room temperature.

4. TO ASSEMBLE TORTE: Using a serrated knife, cut cake lengthwise into three even layers. Place bottom layer on a serving plate; spread with ½ cup Lemon Filling. Top with a second layer; spread with another ½ cup filling. Place last layer on top, cut side down. Spread sides of torte with remaining filling. Press almonds around sides of torte. Refrigerate 1 hour.

5. TO SERVE: Dust top with confectioners' sugar. Using the back of a large knife, score the sugar into a diamond pattern, or sear the score lines by placing a 12-in. metal skewer over a stovetop burner until end is red-hot. Use a kitchen towel to pick up skewer; singe diamond pattern into sugar.

PER SERVING: 222 CAL • 5 G PRO • 43 G CAR • 1 G FIBER • 4 G FAT (1 G SAT FAT) • 3 MG CHOL • 75 MG SOD

cookies

Grownup S'mores

8 Jules Destrooper Crisp Butter
   Wafers (from a 6.1-oz box)

1 bar (3.5 oz) Ghirardelli Intense
   Dark Chocolate
8 marshmallows

1. For each s'more, top 1 wafer with 2 squares of chocolate and 2 marshmallows.
2. Microwave on high 10 to 12 seconds or just until marshmallows start to puff up. Top with another wafer.
   Enjoy warm.

DIFFERENT TAKES

- Substitute a bar of Ghirardelli Espresso Escape Chocolate for the citrus bar.
- Sprinkle English toffee bits on the chocolate before adding marshmallows.
- Coarsely chop cooled s'mores and stir into your favorite ice cream.

PER S'MORE: 270 CAL • 3 G PRO • 41 G CAR • 2 G FIBER • 12 G FAT (7 G SAT FAT) • 9 MG CHOL • 80 MG SOD

Chewy Chocolate Sandwich Cookies

MAKES 34 COOKIES
(17 SANDWICHES)
ACTIVE: 20 MIN / TOTAL: 45 MIN

2 bars (4 oz each) bittersweet
    chocolate, broken into 1-in. pieces
⅔ cup sugar
2 large eggs
2 Tbsp butter, softened
1 tsp vanilla extract

¼ cup all-purpose flour
¼ tsp each baking powder and salt
½ cup mini–semisweet chocolate
    chips
Mint or Coffee Buttercream Frosting
    (recipe follows)

1. Heat oven to 350°F. Line baking sheets with nonstick foil or parchment paper. Put chocolate in large glass bowl. Microwave on high 1 minute, stirring every 20 seconds, until chocolate is melted and smooth.

2. Stir in sugar, eggs, butter and vanilla; mix well. Stir in flour, baking powder and salt until blended. Stir in mini-chips.

3. Drop level tablespoons 1½ in. apart onto prepared baking sheets. Bake 10 minutes or until cookies are puffed and set. Cool on baking sheet 2 minutes before removing to wire rack to cool completely.

4. For each sandwich, spread 1 Tbsp buttercream frosting onto bottom of cookie; press another cookie on top. Refrigerate in an airtight container with wax paper between layers.

Buttercream Frosting

MAKES 1½ CUPS

3 oz cream cheese, softened
2 Tbsp butter, softened
2 cups confectioners' sugar

1 Tbsp milk
¼ tsp vanilla extract

Beat ingredients in medium bowl with electric mixer until smooth. Then beat on high speed 1 minute or until fluffy.

MINT: Use ¼ tsp peppermint extract instead of vanilla; add a few drops of green food color.
COFFEE: Dissolve 1 Tbsp instant coffee in 1 Tbsp hot water; add instead of milk.

PER SANDWICH COOKIE: 208 CAL • 2 G PRO • 30 G CAR • 1 G FIBER • 10 G FAT (6 G SAT FAT) • 35 MG CHOL • 80 MG SOD

Ultimate Chocolate Chunk Cookies

MAKES 30 / ACTIVE: 20 MIN
TOTAL: 45 MIN

2 sticks (1 cup) unsalted butter, softened
1 cup packed brown sugar
½ cup granulated sugar
2 tsp vanilla extract
2 large eggs
1 tsp each baking soda and salt
1½ cups all-purpose flour
2 cups old-fashioned oats
1¼ cups sweetened flaked coconut
2 bars (4 oz each) semisweet chocolate, cut in ½-in. chunks
1 cup coarsely chopped toasted pecans

1. Heat oven to 375°F. Beat butter, sugars and vanilla in a large bowl with electric mixer until fluffy. Beat in eggs, baking soda and salt until blended. On low speed, beat in flour just until blended.

2. Stir in oats, 1 cup of the flaked coconut, all of the chocolate chunks and chopped pecans. Using 2 Tbsp dough for each cookie, drop mounds 2 in. apart onto ungreased baking sheets. Sprinkle tops with the rest of the coconut.

3. Bake 11 to 13 minutes until golden on bottoms and around edges. Cool on baking sheet 2 minutes before removing to wire rack to cool completely.

PER COOKIE: 224 CAL • 3 G PRO • 26 G CAR • 2 G FIBER • 13 G FAT (7 G SAT FAT) • 30 MG CHOL • 137 MG SOD

Devil's Food Chocolate Chunk Cookies

PLANNING TIP:
Cookies can be stored airtight with wax paper between layers at room temperature up to 3 days.

1 box (18.25 oz) devil's food cake mix
1 stick (½ cup) butter, melted
¼ cup water
1 large egg
2 tsp vanilla extract
1½ cups (9 oz) semisweet chocolate chunks
GARNISH: ¼ cup white baking chips

1. Heat oven to 350°F. Line baking sheets with nonstick foil.
2. Beat cake mix, butter, water, egg and vanilla in a medium bowl with mixer on medium speed 1 minute or until blended. Stir in chocolate chunks.
3. Drop heaping tablespoons dough about 3 in. apart on baking sheets.
4. Bake 12 to 14 minutes until puffed and set (cookies will sink when cool). Cool on pan 2 minutes before transferring to a wire rack to cool completely.
5. GARNISH: Put chips in a small ziptop bag; microwave on high, kneading bag every 10 seconds, until chips are melted. Snip a tip off a corner and drizzle chocolate on cookies. Let set.

PER COOKIE: 175 CAL • 2 G PRO • 24 G CAR • 1 G FIBER • 9 G FAT (5 G SAT FAT) • 20 MG CHOL • 204 MG SOD

Chocolate Chunk Cookies

MAKES 30 / ACTIVE: 19 MIN
TOTAL: 55 MIN

PLANNING TIP:
Refrigerate dough airtight up to
5 days or freeze up to 3 months.
Thaw in refrigerator. Bring to room
temperature before proceeding.
Store cookies airtight with wax paper
between layers up to 1 week at room
temperature or freeze up to 2 months.

2 sticks (1 cup) butter, softened
½ cup each granulated sugar and
　　packed light-brown sugar
2 large eggs
2 tsp vanilla extract
½ tsp baking soda
½ tsp salt
2¼ cups all-purpose flour
2 cups semisweet chocolate chunks

1. Heat oven to 350°F.
2. Beat all ingredients except flour and chocolate chunks in a large bowl with mixer on medium speed 3 to 4 minutes until fluffy. On low speed, gradually add flour; beat just to blend. Stir in chocolate.
3. Drop heaping tablespoons 2 in. apart on ungreased baking sheets.
4. Bake 10 to 12 minutes until browned at edges. Cool on sheet on a wire rack 2 minutes before removing to rack to cool completely.

PER COOKIE: 174 CAL • 2 G PRO • 21 G CAR • 1 G FIBER • 10 G FAT (6 G SAT FAT) • 31 MG CHOL • 129 MG SOD

Tropical Ice Cream Sandwiches

SERVES 1 / ACTIVE: 5 MIN
TOTAL: ABOUT 1 HR

Sandwich ⅓ cup slightly softened pineapple-coconut ice cream and vanilla pizzelle or butter wafer cookies. Roll edge in a 1 Tbsp mixture of chopped macadamia nuts and toasted coconut. Freeze
1 hour or until firm.

PER SERVING: 243 CAL • 4 G PRO • 25 G CAR
1 G FIBER • 15 G FAT (7 G SAT FAT) • 64 MG CHOL
73 MG SOD

Strawberry Ice Cream Sandwiches

Sandwich ⅓ cup slightly softened strawberry ice cream and chocolate or vanilla pizzelle or chocolate or butter wafer cookies. Freeze 1 hour or until firm.

PER SERVING: 132 CAL • 2 G PRO • 18 G CAR
0 G FIBER • 6 G FAT (3 G SAT FAT) • 18 MG CHOL
35 MG SOD

Pistachio Ice Cream Sandwiches

Sandwich ⅓ cup slightly softened pistachio ice cream and vanilla pizzelle or butter wafer cookies. Roll edge in 1 Tbsp chopped pistachios. Freeze 1 hour or until firm.

PER SERVING: 203 CAL • 5 G PRO • 17 G CAR
1 G FIBER • 13 G FAT (4 G SAT FAT) • 25 MG CHOL
48 MG SOD

Minted Macaroons

MAKES 46 / ACTIVE: 20 MIN
TOTAL: 1 HR 10 MIN

1 can (14 oz) sweetened condensed milk
(not evaporated milk)
1 bag (14 oz) sweetened flaked coconut
    (5⅓ cups)
1½ cups pastel-color mint-flavor
    chocolate lentils
2 large egg whites, at room temperature

1. Heat oven to 325°F. Line baking sheets with foil. Coat with nonstick spray and dust with flour.

2. Mix condensed milk, coconut and ¾ cup chocolate lentils in a large bowl.

3. Beat egg whites in a small to medium bowl with mixer on high speed until stiff peaks form when beaters are lifted. Fold into coconut mixture.

4. Drop level tablespoons of mixture about 1 in. apart on prepared baking sheets. Place 3 to 4 chocolate lentils on top of each.

5. Bake 14 to 16 minutes until macaroons are lightly toasted. Slide foil onto a wire rack; cool macaroons completely before peeling off foil.

PER MACAROON: 103 CAL • 2 G PRO • 13 G CAR • 1 G FIBER • 5 G FAT (3 G SAT FAT) • 4 MG CHOL • 41 MG SOD

Lemon-Ginger Cookie Stacks

SERVES 8 / ACTIVE: 8 MIN
TOTAL: 8 MIN
(PLUS 2 HR CHILLING)

1 container (6 oz) lowfat lemon
   yogurt
1½ cups frozen reduced-calorie
   whipped topping, thawed
32 thin ginger cookies (from a
   5.25-oz box)
GARNISH: raspberries, strips of
   crystallized ginger

1. Stir lemon yogurt in large bowl until smooth. Fold in whipped topping.

2. Put 8 ginger cookies, right side up, on a tray. Spoon 1 level tablespoon lemon cream on top of each cookie, then top with another cookie; repeat twice.

3. Place a dollop of remaining lemon cream on top of each. Refrigerate about 2 hours just until cookies soften slightly. Garnish tops with raspberries and crystallized ginger.

PER SERVING: 143 CAL • 2 G PRO • 19 G CAR • 1 G FIBER • 6 G FAT (3 G SAT FAT) • 1 MG CHOL • 115 MG SOD

Lemon Crisps

MAKES 42 / ACTIVE: 20 MIN
TOTAL: 1 HR

1 stick (½ cup) unsalted butter, softened
¾ cup sugar
1 large egg
1½ Tbsp each grated lemon zest and lemon juice
½ tsp vanilla extract
½ tsp baking powder

¼ tsp each baking soda and salt
1¼ cups all-purpose flour

LEMON DRIZZLE
1 cup confectioners' sugar
4 to 6 tsp lemon juice

Yellow nonpareils (optional)

1. Heat oven to 350°F. Beat butter and sugar 2 minutes or until fluffy. Beat in egg, lemon zest and juice, vanilla, baking powder, baking soda and salt until well mixed. On low speed, beat in flour just until blended.

2. Drop rounded teaspoons 1½ in. apart on ungreased baking sheets. Bake 10 to 12 minutes until edges are lightly golden. Cool on baking sheet 1 minute before removing to wire rack to cool completely.

3. DRIZZLE: Stir ingredients in small bowl until blended. Drizzle over cookies; sprinkle with nonpareils, if desired.

PER COOKIE: 60 CAL • 1 G PRO • 9 G CAR • 0 G FIBER • 2 G FAT (1 G SAT FAT) • 11 MG CHOL • 30 MG SOD

Soft Ginger-Apple Cookies

MAKES 36 / ACTIVE: 25 MIN
TOTAL: 1 HR 10 MIN

1 stick (½ cup) unsalted butter,
　softened
1 cup packed light-brown sugar
½ cup unsweetened applesauce
1 large egg
1½ tsp ground ginger
1 tsp baking soda

½ tsp salt
2¾ cups all-purpose flour
¼ cup finely chopped crystallized
　ginger
Apple Buttercream Frosting
　(see below)
Slivered crystallized ginger

1. Heat oven to 350°F. Beat butter and sugar in large bowl with electric mixer until fluffy. Beat in remaining ingredients, except flour and crystallized ginger, until blended (mixture will look curdled).
2. With mixer on low speed, add flour and beat just until blended; stir in crystallized ginger.
3. Drop level tablespoons 2 in. apart on ungreased baking sheets. Bake 10 to 12 minutes until tops look dry. Cool on baking sheet 1 minute before removing to wire rack to cool completely.
4. Spread a rounded teaspoon buttercream frosting on each cooled cookie. Sprinkle with slivered crystallized ginger. Refrigerate in an airtight container with wax paper between layers.

Apple Buttercream Frosting

MAKES 1½ CUPS

3 oz cream cheese, softened
2 Tbsp butter, softened
2 cups confectioners' sugar

1 to 2 Tbsp apple juice (until
　spreadable)
¼ tsp vanilla extract

Beat ingredients in medium bowl with electric mixer until smooth. Then beat on high speed 1 minute or until fluffy.

PER COOKIE: 124 CAL • 1 G PRO • 22 G CAR • 0 G FIBER • 4 G FAT (2 G SAT FAT) • 15 MG CHOL • 81 MG SOD

Stuck-on-You-Baby Kisses

MAKES 36 / ACTIVE: 20 MIN
TOTAL: 3 HR (INCLUDES COOLING)

PLANNING TIP:
Store individual meringues airtight at room temperature up to 1 month. Sandwich with jam no more than 30 minutes before serving.

3 large egg whites
¼ tsp cream of tartar
¾ cup sugar
½ tsp almond extract
¼ tsp liquid red food color
3 Tbsp strawberry jam
GARNISH: fresh strawberries

1. Position racks to divide oven in thirds. Heat to 225°F. Line 2 baking sheets with nonstick foil.
2. Beat egg whites with cream of tartar in a large bowl with mixer on medium speed until soft peaks form when beaters are lifted.
3. On high speed, gradually add sugar and beat about 8 minutes until stiff, white, glossy peaks form and mixture no longer feels grainy. Beat in almond extract and food color until thoroughly blended.
4. Spoon into a large ziptop bag, snip ½ in. off a corner and pipe 72 small mounds (each about 1 in. across) 1 in. apart on baking sheets.
5. Bake 1¾ hour or until meringues feel firm. Turn off oven; leave meringues in oven 1 hour or overnight, until kisses are dry and crisp all the way through. Peel off foil.
6. Shortly before serving: Put ¼ tsp jam on bottom of 1 meringue; sandwich with another meringue. Repeat with remaining meringues and jam.

PER SANDWICHED KISSES: 22 CAL • 0 G PRO • 5 G CAR • 0 G FIBER • 0 G FAT (0 G SAT FAT) • 0 MG CHOL • 5 MG SOD

The Ultimate Nutty Cookie

MAKES 60 / ACTIVE: 30 MIN
TOTAL: 1¼ HR

6 NutRageous candy bars (1.8 oz each)
3 Butterfinger candy bars (2.1 oz each)
2 sticks (1 cup) butter, softened
1 cup packed light-brown sugar
½ cup creamy peanut butter
¼ cup granulated sugar
2 tsp vanilla extract
2 large eggs
1 tsp baking soda
2⅓ cups all-purpose flour
1½ cups honey-roasted peanuts and
  cashews

1. Heat oven to 350°F. Cut 3 NutRageous bars and the Butterfinger bars into ⅓-in. chunks (Butterfingers will
    shatter; that's OK). Set aside.

3. Beat butter, brown sugar, peanut butter, granulated sugar and vanilla in a large bowl with mixer on medium
    speed 1 to 2 minutes until fluffy. Beat in eggs and baking soda until combined. On low speed, beat in flour
    just until blended. Stir in cut-up candy bars and the nuts. Drop rounded tablespoons dough about 2 in.
    apart on ungreased baking sheets. Thinly slice remaining NutRageous bars; place a slice on
    each cookie.

4. Bake 9 to 11 minutes until edges are golden brown. Cool on sheet 2 minutes before removing cookies to a
    wire rack to cool completely.

PER COOKIE: 138 CAL • 3 G PRO • 14 G CAR • 1 G FIBER • 8 G FAT (3 G SAT FAT) • 15 MG CHOL • 91 MG SOD

Flourless Peanut Butter Cookies

MAKES 48 / ACTIVE: 25 MIN
TOTAL: 55 MIN

2 cups creamy peanut butter
2 cups packed light-brown sugar
2 large eggs
2 tsp baking soda
1 cup coarsely chopped cocktail
  peanuts

GANACHE
½ cup heavy cream
1 cup bittersweet chocolate chips
GARNISH: chopped peanuts

1. Heat oven to 350°F. Beat peanut butter, sugar, eggs and baking soda in large bowl with electric mixer
    2 minutes or until smooth and blended. Stir in chopped peanuts.
2. Drop level tablespoons 2 in. apart, flat side down, onto ungreased baking sheets. Bake, one sheet at a time,
    10 minutes or until cookies are puffed and slightly golden. Cool 5 minutes on baking sheet; remove to wire
    racks to cool completely.
3. GANACHE: Microwave cream in glass bowl on high 1 minute or until it just begins to simmer. Add chocolate
    chips; let stand 2 minutes. Stir until chocolate is melted and smooth; spread over half of cookie top and
    sprinkle with chopped peanuts. If ganache begins to firm up, microwave a few seconds at a time until easy
    to spread. Let set at room temperature.

PER COOKIE: 141 CAL • 4 G PRO • 14 G CAR • 1 G FIBER • 9 G FAT (3 G SAT FAT) • 12 MG CHOL • 113 MG SOD

Black-&-White Snowballs

2 cups of any of the following:
chocolate crisp rice cereal, sweetened
flaked coconut, mini–chocolate chips,
chopped chocolate-covered almonds,
chopped glazed walnuts, crushed
chocolate wafers, crushed almond
crisp cookies
1 pint light vanilla, chocolate or coffee
ice cream

1. Place desired coating on a sheet of wax paper. Place a foil-lined baking sheet in freezer.

2. Roll scoops of ice cream (about 1¾-in.) in coating; arrange on baking sheet in freezer.

TIP: Store frozen ice cream balls in an airtight container in freezer for up to 2 weeks.

PER SERVING: 63 CAL • 1 G PRO • 12 G CAR • 0 G FIBER • 1 G FAT (1 G SAT FAT) • 6 MG CHOL • 60 MG SOD

Stained-Glass Tulip Cookies

MAKES 32 / ACTIVE: 30 MIN
TOTAL: 3 HR (INCLUDES AT LEAST
30 MIN CHILLING DOUGH)

3 sticks (1½ cups) butter, softened
1 cup sugar
1 large egg
2 tsp baking powder
1 tsp each ground ginger and
   vanilla extract

½ tsp salt
4 cups all-purpose flour
30 lollipop sticks
About 50 Life Savers or Jolly Ranchers
   hard candies, assorted colors, each
   color crushed separately

1. Beat butter and sugar in a large bowl with mixer on medium speed until pale and fluffy. On low speed, beat in next 5 ingredients to combine. Gradually beat in flour until blended.

2. Divide dough in half; shape each into a 1-in.-thick disk. Wrap and refrigerate 30 minutes, or until firm enough to roll.

3. Heat oven to 350°F. Line baking sheets with foil; coat with nonstick spray. You'll need a 3¼ x 2½-in. tulip cookie cutter.

4. On lightly floured wax paper, with floured rolling pin, roll out 1 disk dough (keep other refrigerated) to ¼-in. thick. Cut out tulips. Place 2 in. apart on lined baking sheets, with tops of tulips along long edges of sheet. Insert a lollipop stick in bottom of each. Using a small, pointed knife, cut "windows" in tulips. Reroll and cut scraps twice. Repeat with remaining dough.

5. Bake 1 sheet at a time 8 minutes, or until just barely tinged brown at edges. Using a small spoon, fill cutouts with candy until level with top of dough. Brush off stray bits. Bake 4 minutes, or until candy melts.

6. Cool on sheet on a wire rack 7 to 10 minutes until "glass" cools and hardens. Transfer to wire rack to cool completely.

PER COOKIE: 210 CAL • 2 G PRO • 26 G CAR • 0 G FIBER • 9 G FAT (5 G SAT FAT) • 32 MG CHOL • 167 MG SOD

Strawberry-Almond Candy Kiss Cookies

MAKES 60 / ACTIVE: 45 MIN
TOTAL: 1 HR 20 MIN

2½ cups sliced almonds, toasted as
    pkg directs and cooled
½ cup granulated sugar
1 cup packed dark-brown sugar
2 sticks (1 cup) butter, softened
2 large eggs
1 tsp almond extract

½ tsp baking powder
2¾ cups all-purpose flour
2 large egg whites, beaten with a fork
60 Strawberry Cream Hershey's
    Kisses (from two 9.2-oz bags;
    see Note)

1. Heat oven to 350°F. Coat baking sheets with nonstick spray.
2. In food processor, pulse 1 cup almonds and the granulated sugar until nuts are ground. Scrape into a small bowl and reserve.
3. In processor, pulse remaining 1½ cups almonds and the brown sugar until nuts are ground. Scrape into a large bowl and add butter, eggs, almond extract and baking powder. Beat with mixer on medium speed until fluffy. On low speed, gradually add flour and beat just until blended.
4. Roll level tablespoons dough into 1¼-in. balls. Dip each into beaten egg whites, then roll in reserved almond-sugar mixture. Place about 1 in. apart on prepared baking sheets. Press index finger ¼ of the way down the center of each to make an indent.
5. Bake 9 minutes, or until light-brown around edges. Place sheet on wire rack and immediately place a Kiss in each indent (Kisses will melt slightly). Remove cookies to rack to cool completely.

NOTE: Hershey's Hugs or other Hershey's Kisses can be substituted.

PER COOKIE: 119 CAL • 2 G PRO • 13 G CAR • 0 G FIBER • 7 G FAT (3 G SAT FAT) • 16 MG CHOL • 48 MG SOD

mousses & puddings

Mini-Mochaccino Puddings

4 cups milk
⅔ cup sugar
¼ cup cornstarch
2 Tbsp unsweetened cocoa
1 Tbsp instant espresso powder
⅛ tsp salt
8 oz bittersweet chocolate, broken up
1 Tbsp vanilla extract
1 cup heavy cream
2 Tbsp confectioners' sugar
GARNISH: ground cinnamon,
  chocolate curls (optional)

1. Whisk milk, sugar, cornstarch, cocoa, espresso powder and salt in a large saucepan until blended. Bring to a boil over medium-high heat, stirring often with a whisk and making sure to reach into corners of saucepan.
2. Boil 1 minute, whisking, until thickened. Remove from heat; stir in chocolate and vanilla until chocolate is melted and mixture is smooth.
3. Pour into twelve 3- to 4-oz espresso or other small cups or glasses. Cover with wax paper; refrigerate at least 1 hour or until firm.
4. TO SERVE: Beat cream and confectioners' sugar until very soft peaks form. Place dollops over tops of pudding. Sift ground cinnamon through a strainer to garnish; add chocolate curls, if desired.

PER SERVING: 274 CAL • 4 G PRO • 30 G CAR • 2 G FIBER • 17 G FAT (10 G SAT FAT) • 36 MG CHOL • 66 MG SOD

Chocolate Espresso Pudding

2 cups milk
5 Tbsp sugar
2 Tbsp cornstarch
1 Tbsp unsweetened cocoa
Pinch salt
1 bar (3.5 oz) dark chocolate with
    espresso (such as Ghirardelli
    Espresso Escape), broken up
1 tsp vanilla extract
GARNISH: lightly sweetened whipped
    cream, espresso beans, cinnamon

1. Whisk milk, sugar, cornstarch, cocoa and salt in a medium saucepan to blend. Bring to a boil over medium-high heat. Stir often with a whisk, going into corners of saucepan.

2. Boil 1 minute, whisking, until thickened. Remove from heat; stir in chocolate and vanilla until chocolate melts and mixture is blended.

3. Scrape into a bowl. Cover surface directly with plastic wrap. Chill at least 2 hours or until cold. Spoon into small cups or bowls; garnish.

PER SERVING: 279 CAL • 5 G PRO • 40 G CAR • 2 G FIBER • 13 G FAT (8 G SAT FAT) • 17 MG CHOL • 97 MG SOD

Cookies & Cream Parfaits

SERVES 4 / ACTIVE: 10 MIN
TOTAL: 1 HR 10 MIN (INCLUDES CHILLING)

1 box (3.4 oz) cook-and-serve chocolate
  pudding and pie filling
2 cups milk
1 cup whipped topping
2 soft chocolate cookies (we used
  Archway)
GARNISH: chocolate curls

1. You'll need four 6-oz dessert glasses. Prepare pudding as package directs, using milk. After cooking, scrape into a medium bowl and press plastic wrap directly onto surface of pudding. Refrigerate pudding until cold, at least 1 hour.

2. TO MAKE PARFAITS: Put ¼ cup pudding into each glass. Top each with 2 Tbsp nondairy whipped topping, then crumble ½ a cookie onto each. Top with ¼ cup more pudding and 2 Tbsp topping. Garnish if desired.

PER SERVING: 280 CAL • 5 G PRO • 42 G CAR • 1 G FIBER • 9 G FAT (7 G SAT FAT) • 14 MG CHOL • 187 MG SOD

Mousse Cake

2½ cups heavy (whipping) cream
8 oz white baking chocolate, chopped
1 box (17.28 oz) Banquet Dessert
   Bakes Chocolate Silk Pie mix
2 Tbsp sugar
GARNISH: cocoa powder (optional)

1. Heat ¼ cup cream and the chocolate, stirring until chocolate melts. Transfer to a large bowl. Let cool.
2. Coat an 8-in. springform pan with nonstick spray. Coat sides with 1 Tbsp crust mix. Prepare rest of crust as box directs. Press over bottom.
3. Beat 1¼ cups cream with mixer on high speed until stiff. Stir a big dollop into white chocolate mixture; fold in remaining whipped cream.
4. Prepare pie filling as box directs. Spoon filling and white chocolate mousse into separate gallon ziptop bags. Cut ¾ in. off a corner of each. Pipe a ring of pie filling around edge of pan. Pipe a ring of mousse next to pie filling. Repeat until crust is covered.
5. Reverse rings on next layer, starting with mousse, then repeat first two layers. Cover directly with plastic wrap; press to smooth top layer and remove any air bubbles. Refrigerate or freeze 3 hours to set.
6. TO SERVE: Remove pan sides; place cake on serving plate. Beat remaining 1 cup cream and the sugar until soft peaks form. Spread on top of cake; dust with cocoa powder, if desired. Serve cold or frozen.

DIFFERENT TAKES
• Sprinkle shaved chocolate between each of the layers.
• Flavor the pie filling with liqueur.
• Scatter some fresh raspberries between each layer.

PER SERVING: 334 CAL • 4 G PRO • 31 G CAR • 1 G FIBER • 22 G FAT (14 G SAT FAT) • 54 MG CHOL • 170 MG SOD

Chocolate–Peanut Butter Parfaits

SERVES 8 / ACTIVE: 20 MIN
TOTAL: 1 HR 20 MIN (INCLUDES
1 HR CHILLING)

1 cup heavy (whipping) cream
¾ cup peanut butter chips
1½ cups prepared chocolate pudding
GARNISH: whipped cream and peanut
   butter chips

1. Heat ½ cup cream in a medium glass bowl in microwave until steaming hot. Add chips; stir with a whisk until melted and smooth. Whisk in remaining cream. Refrigerate until cold.

2. Beat with mixer just until soft peaks form (don't overbeat).

3. Spread 1 heaping Tbsp peanut butter mousse into bottom of each of 8 small (about ½-cup capacity) stemmed glasses. Spread with 1 heaping Tbsp chocolate pudding. Repeat layers once. Garnish and serve, or cover and refrigerate (without garnish) up to 1 day.

DIFFERENT TAKES

- Replace peanut butter chips with butterscotch chips.
- Instead of layering in glasses, spoon alternating dollops into small dessert bowls, then swirl mixtures together with the tip of a knife.
- Sprinkle crumbled chocolate wafer cookies between layers and on top.

PER SERVING: 281 CAL • 6 G PRO • 21 G CAR • 0 G FIBER • 19 G FAT (13 G SAT FAT) • 42 MG CHOL • 120 MG SOD

Frozen Mousse Triangles

SERVES 9 / ACTIVE: 10 MIN
TOTAL: 10 MIN (PLUS FREEZING
OVERNIGHT)

4½ chocolate graham crackers
1¼ cups milk
¼ tsp mint extract
2 boxes (2.8 oz each) milk chocolate
   European Style mousse mix
1 cup miniature marshmallows

1. Line an 8-in. square pan with foil, letting foil extend about 2 in. over ends. Arrange graham crackers over bottom, cutting to fit.
2. Stir milk and mint extract in large bowl. Add mousse mix and prepare as package directs.
3. Spoon 1 cup mousse over graham crackers. Evenly sprinkle with marshmallows and spread with remaining mousse. Cover and freeze overnight.
4. Lift foil by ends onto cutting board. Cut in 9 squares, then in half diagonally to make triangles. Remove from foil.

PER 2 TRIANGLES: 147 CAL • 3 G PRO • 26 G CAR • 1 G FIBER • 4 G FAT (3 G SAT FAT) • 5 MG CHOL • 137 MG SOD

Baked Rice Pudding

2 large eggs, plus 1 large egg yolk

2½ cups whole milk

½ cup sugar

½ tsp each almond and vanilla extract

1 pouch (8.8 oz) 90-second microwave
  long-grain rice

¾ cup dried cranberries, preferably
  orange-flavor

1. Heat oven to 325°F. Put six 6-oz ramekins or custard cups on a rimmed baking sheet.
2. Whisk eggs, egg yolk, milk, sugar and extracts in a medium bowl until blended. Heat rice in microwave as package directs.
3. Put ¼ cup hot rice and 2 Tbsp cranberries into each ramekin, then add the egg mixture (about ½ cup to each).
4. Bake 35 minutes, or until a knife inserted in centers comes out clean. Best served warm.

PER SERVING: 271 CAL • 7 G PRO • 46 G CAR • 2 G FIBER • 6 G FAT (3 G SAT FAT) • 120 MG CHOL • 81 MG SOD

Orange Rice Pudding

⅔ cup Arborio rice

8 cups water

Pinch of salt

4 cups protein-fortified fat-free milk

3 Tbsp each packed light brown sugar
   and granulated sugar

1 tsp vanilla extract

½ tsp grated orange zest

¼ tsp ground cardamom or
   cinnamon

1. Place rice in sieve. Rinse under cold water, stirring with fingers, to remove excess surface starch. Place in a 5-qt saucepan with water and salt, and bring to a boil over high heat. Reduce heat to medium and boil 7 minutes, or until tender. Drain rice; return to pot.

2. Stir milk and sugars into rice, stirring to dissolve sugars. Bring to a boil over medium-high heat. Reduce heat to medium-low to maintain a slow simmer. Simmer, stirring frequently at first and constantly toward the end, for about 25 minutes, or until rice doubles in size, is very soft and tender, and milk has the consistency of heavy cream (mixture will be very liquidy).

3. Pour into a bowl; stir in vanilla, orange zest and cardamom. Cover surface of pudding with plastic wrap to prevent a skin from forming. Let cool. Refrigerate until chilled, about 4 hours, before serving.

PER SERVING: 158 CAL • 7 G PRO • 31 G CAR • 0 G FIBER • 1 G FAT (0 G SAT FAT) • 2 MG CHOL • 92 MG SOD

Orange Rice Pudding Parfaits

For each parfait, spoon ¼ cup orange rice pudding into a glass, then top with 3 orange sections, 1 Tbsp thawed reduced-calorie whipped topping and 1 tsp fat-free butterscotch caramel topping. Repeat layers.

PER PARFAIT: 242 CAL • 7 G PRO • 51 G CAR • 1 G FIBER • 2 G FAT (1 G SAT FAT) • 2 MG CHOL • 133 MG SOD

Raspberry-Lemon
Custard Cakes

SERVES 8 / ACTIVE: 15 MIN
TOTAL: 45 MIN

½ pint raspberries
4 large egg whites
3 large egg yolks
¾ cup granulated sugar
2 Tbsp all-purpose flour
1½ tsp raspberry extract
1 tsp lemon zest
¼ cup lemon juice
1 cup milk
Confectioners' sugar for dusting

1. Fill a roasting pan with ½ in. of hot tap water; place in center of oven. Heat oven to 350°F. You'll need eight 6-oz custard cups; place 4 or 5 raspberries on bottom of each.

2. Beat egg whites in a medium bowl with mixer on medium speed until foamy. Beat in 2 Tbsp of the sugar until stiff, shiny peaks form when beaters are lifted.

3. With same beaters (no need to wash), beat yolks and remaining sugar in a large bowl until mixture is light; beat in flour, extract, lemon zest and juice. Gradually beat in milk. Using a wire whisk, gently fold egg whites into yolk mixture just until combined. Divide batter among prepared cups (cups should be filled to the top). Place cups in hot water in roasting pan.

4. Bake until puddings are puffed and golden brown on top, about 24 minutes. Serve puddings warm or at room temperature, with confectioners' sugar and remaining berries.

PER SERVING: 138 CAL • 4 G PRO • 25 G CAR • 1 G FIBER • 3 G FAT (1 G SAT FAT) • 80 MG CHOL • 43 MG SOD

Mango-Cherry Semifreddo with Tart Red Cherry Sauce

SERVES 10 / ACTIVE: 35 MIN
TOTAL: 24 HR (INCLUDES FREEZING)

SEMIFREDDO

1½ cups pitted fresh or frozen tart red cherries

3 ripe mangoes, peeled, pitted and cut in chunks (3 cups)

3 Tbsp honey

½ cup nonfat sour cream

5 large eggs, at room temperature

½ cup sugar

CHERRY SAUCE

1½ cups pitted fresh or frozen tart red cherries

¼ cup each sugar and water

GARNISH: diced mango

PLANNING TIP: You can make and freeze the semifreddo and make and refrigerate the sauce up to 1 week ahead.

1. SEMIFREDDO: Cut cherries into small pieces; spread in a single layer on a foil-lined baking sheet and freeze until very hard. You'll need an 8-in. springform pan lined with nonstick foil. Place pan in freezer while preparing semifreddo.

2. Purée mangoes and honey in blender until smooth. Transfer to a large bowl; whisk in sour cream until blended.

3. Put eggs and sugar in a large, heatproof bowl set over a saucepan of simmering water. With mixer on high speed, beat mixture until thick, pale and tripled in volume, about 10 minutes, or until mixture registers 160°F on an instant-read thermometer. Remove from heat and fold into mango mixture.

4. Fold half of the frozen cherries into mixture and pour into prepared springform pan. Scatter remaining frozen cherries over top of batter. Freeze 24 hours or until solid.

5. CHERRY SAUCE: In a medium saucepan, bring ingredients for sauce to a boil; gently boil 6 minutes. Pour mixture into a blender and purée. Pour into a container and refrigerate until serving.

6. TO SERVE: Remove sides from springform pan. Cut into wedges and place on plates. Let stand until slightly softened. Serve with cherry sauce and diced mango.

PER SERVING WITH 2 TBSP SAUCE: 190 CAL • 5 G PRO • 39 G CAR • 2 G FIBER • 3 G FAT (1 G SAT FAT) • 106 MG CHOL • 45 MG SOD

Pavlova with Summer Fruit

SERVES 8 / ACTIVE: 30 MIN
TOTAL: 6 HR (INCLUDES COOLING)

4 large egg whites, at room
  temperature
1 cup granulated sugar, preferably
  superfine
1 tsp vanilla extract
1 Tbsp cornstarch

1 tsp white vinegar
½ cup nonfat sour cream
2 cups reduced-calorie whipped
  topping
6 cups diced mixed fresh fruit

PLANNING TIP: You can make the meringue up to 2 days ahead; store in an airtight container at room temperature.

1. Heat oven to 300°F. Line a baking sheet with nonstick foil.
2. Beat egg whites with mixer on medium speed until soft peaks form when beaters are lifted. Gradually add sugar, 1 Tbsp at a time, until incorporated. Scrape down sides of bowl, then continue to beat on high speed 7 minutes or until stiff, white, glossy peaks form and mixture no longer feels grainy. Beat in vanilla extract.
3. Sift cornstarch over beaten whites and drizzle with vinegar; fold in with a rubber spatula until incorporated.
4. Mound meringue on prepared baking sheet and shape into a 6 ½-in. round using a metal offset spatula. Indent the top of the mound with spatula to form a slight hollow.
5. Place in oven; reduce oven temperature to 250°F. Bake 1 hour. Turn off oven and completely cool in oven, about 4 hours. The meringue will crack in several places; this is how it should be.
6. Using a small knife, carefully cut around top of meringue, letting crisp pieces fall into the middle of the shell, forming an indentation.
7. In a large bowl, fold sour cream into nondairy topping.
8. TO SERVE: Spoon 3 cups of the fruit in middle of meringue. Top with sour cream mixture, then remaining fruit. Serve immediately.

PER SERVING: 225 CAL • 4 G PRO • 47 G CAR • 2 G FIBER • 2 G FAT (2 G SAT FAT) • 0 MG CHOL • 42 MG SOD

Individual Summer Puddings

SERVES 4 / ACTIVE: 45 MIN
TOTAL: 24 HR
(INCLUDES CHILLING)

½ pint each red raspberries and
fresh red currants, on stems
(if currants are unavailable, use
1 pint raspberries)
½ pint blackberries, halved
⅓ cup sugar
2 Tbsp each black currant liqueur
(cassis) and water
2 Tbsp strawberry or raspberry jam

2 strips lemon zest (2 in. each),
removed with a vegetable peeler
½ pint strawberries, diced
13 slices firm-textured, cholesterol-
free white bread, crusts removed
GARNISH: reduced-calorie whipped
topping, assorted berries, mint
leaves

PLANNING TIP: You can assemble and chill puddings up to 3 days before serving.

1. You'll need four 8-oz (1-cup) ramekins or custard cups. Line each with plastic wrap, letting wrap extend 3 in. beyond tops of ramekins.

2. Bring raspberries, currants (removed from stems), blackberries, sugar, cassis, water, jam and lemon zest to a boil in a saucepan. Lower heat and simmer 2 minutes, or until berries have released their juices but still hold their shape. Remove from heat; stir in strawberries and cool to room temperature. Discard lemon zest.

3. Using a 3-in. round cookie cutter, cut out 8 bread rounds. Trim 4 to fit on bottoms of prepared ramekins; reserve remaining rounds. Line sides of ramekins to within ½ in. from tops with remaining bread slices, cutting bread to fit and leaving no gaps.

4. Spoon fruit mixture into lined ramekins to fill (reserve remaining fruit mixture). Top with rest of bread rounds.

5. Seal with plastic wrap overhang, then wrap tops with foil. Place ramekins in a baking dish. Place a weight (like a can of tomatoes) on top of each ramekin to weigh down. Refrigerate overnight or up to 3 days.

6. Purée reserved fruit mixture in blender; scrape through a fine-mesh sieve to remove seeds. Refrigerate.

7. TO SERVE: Unwrap ramekins. Carefully lift out puddings by plastic wrap; invert onto serving plates and remove wrap. Brush puddings with reserved fruit purée to even out color. Top with a dollop of whipped topping and garnish with berries, as shown.

PER SERVING: 251 CAL • 4 G PRO • 57 G CAR • 6 G FIBER • 2 G FAT (0 G SAT FAT) • 0 MG CHOL • 171 MG SOD

Frozen Lowfat Strawberry Swirl Terrine

SERVES 16 / ACTIVE: 20 MIN
TOTAL: 20 MIN (PLUS AT LEAST
4 HR FREEZING)

PLANNING TIP:
Can be made through Step 3 up to
2 weeks ahead.

1 tub (1.75 quart) light vanilla ice cream,
   slightly softened
4 (4 oz each) lowfat ice cream &
   strawberry sorbet swirl bars (we used
   The Skinny Cow)
1 jar (15.5 oz) strawberry ice cream
   topping
GARNISH: fresh strawberries

1. Line an 8 x 4-in. loaf pan with foil, letting foil extend at least 3 in. above pan sides.
2. Spread 2 cups vanilla ice cream in lined pan. Remove sticks from ice cream bars. Cut bars horizontally in half. Lay 4 halves, cut side up, in a row on top of ice cream.
3. Repeat layers as above. Spread remaining vanilla ice cream firmly over top. Cover airtight with extending foil and freeze at least 4 hours until firm.
4. TO SERVE: Unfold foil on top and, holding foil, lift terrine from pan and invert onto a serving platter. Cut in 16 slices. Spoon about 2 Tbsp strawberry topping on each serving plate, top with a slice and garnish with strawberries.

PER SERVING: 202 CAL • 3 G PRO • 39 G CAR • 0 G FIBER • 5 G FAT (3 G SAT FAT) • 18 MG CHOL • 58 MG SOD

Frozen Black-&-White Crème Brûlée

SERVES 6 / ACTIVE: 20 MIN
TOTAL: 24 HR (INCLUDES FREEZING OVERNIGHT)

1½ cups lowfat chocolate sorbet,
    slightly softened
1 pint lowfat vanilla bean ice cream,
    slightly softened
¼ cup fat-free caramel sauce
GARNISH: chocolate shavings
    (optional)

1. Place six ¾-cup oval or round crème brûlée ramekins in the freezer for 1 hour to chill thoroughly. Spread
    ¼ cup chocolate sorbet into an even layer in each ramekin. Freeze until firm.
2. Top each sorbet layer with ⅓ cup ice cream, spreading into a smooth layer. Cover with nonstick foil. Freeze
    ramekins overnight.
3. To finish, drizzle a thin layer of caramel sauce over each ramekin. Immediately return to freezer. Garnish
    with chocolate shavings, if desired.

PER SERVING: 175 CAL • 3 G PRO • 36 G CAR • 2 G FIBER • 2 G FAT (1 G SAT FAT) • 3 MG CHOL • 106 MG SOD

Tropical Chiffon Pie

⅔ cup boiling water

1 box (3 oz) pineapple-flavor gelatin

2 cups ice cubes

2 cups frozen reduced-calorie whipped topping, thawed

1 tsp grated lime zest

1¼ cups chopped mango and papaya

1 (6-oz) ready-to-fill reduced-fat graham-cracker crust

¼ cup sweetened flaked coconut, toasted (see Note, next page)

1. Stir boiling water into gelatin in large bowl until completely dissolved. Add ice cubes; stir until gelatin begins to thicken, about 1 minute. Remove and discard unmelted ice.
2. Whisk in 1 cup whipped topping and the lime zest. Fold in remaining topping, then the fruit. Spoon into crust. Sprinkle edge of pie with coconut. Refrigerate at least 3 hours until set.

PER SERVING: 195 CAL • 2 G PRO • 33 G CAR • 1 G FIBER • 6 G FAT (3 G SAT FAT) • 0 MG CHOL • 142 MG SOD

Coconut Flan

SERVES 12 / ACTIVE: 15 MIN
TOTAL: 15 MIN (PLUS AT LEAST
2 HR CHILLING)

PLANNING TIP:
Can be made through Step 4 up to
3 days ahead. Cover and refrigerate.
Unmold up to 3 hours before serving.

2 boxes (3 oz each) flan mix
2 cups whole milk
1 can (14 oz) lite coconut milk
1 cup sweetened flaked coconut, toasted
    (see Note)
GARNISH: strips of fresh or dried
    coconut

1. You'll need a round 8 x 2-in. baking dish or pan and a rimmed serving plate.

2. Pour caramel sauce from flan mix into baking dish. Tilt to cover bottom.

3. Prepare both boxes flan mix in a medium saucepan as packages direct, using milk and coconut milk. Remove from heat; stir in coconut.

4. Ladle custard over caramel. Refrigerate at least 2 hours, or overnight.

5. TO UNMOLD: Run a thin knife around edge of flan. Place inverted rimmed serving plate on dish. Holding plate and dish together, carefully turn both over. Lift dish, letting syrup run onto plate. Refrigerate until serving.

NOTE: To toast coconut, spread in a shallow pan or microwave-safe plate. Bake at 350°F or microwave on high, stirring as needed, 5 minutes or until golden.

PER SERVING: 125 CAL • 2 G PRO • 19 G CAR • 0 G FIBER • 5 G FAT (4 G SAT FAT) • 6 MG CHOL • 48 MG SOD

Honey Greek Yogurt Fillo Cups

SERVES 6 / ACTIVE: 25 MIN
TOTAL: 40 MIN

Butter-flavored cooking spray
1 pint strawberries, washed, hulled and sliced
3 Tbsp granulated sugar
¼ tsp vanilla extract
¼ tsp pumpkin pie spice

4 (14 x 9-in.) sheets frozen fillo dough, thawed
1½ cups nonfat Greek yogurt, stirred
4 Tbsp honey or agave nectar
GARNISH: small mint leaves (optional)

1. Heat oven to 350°F. You'll need 6 (5-in.) metal or foil pie pans lightly coated with cooking spray. In bowl, toss strawberries with 1 Tbsp sugar and the vanilla; let stand until juicy. Mix remaining 2 Tbsp sugar and pumpkin pie spice in small cup.

2. Stack fillo sheets; cut in half lengthwise, then crosswise into thirds (24 pieces total).

3. To make fillo cups (4 pieces per cup): Place 1 piece fillo in each pie pan; lightly coat with cooking spray. Sprinkle with some of the spiced sugar. Layer a second piece of fillo in each pan, slightly off center of the first; coat with spray and sprinkle with spiced sugar. Finish building the cups with 2 more layers of fillo, coated with spray and sprinkled with spiced sugar, each layer slightly off center of the previous.

4. Bake 10 minutes or until cups are golden and crisp. Carefully lift shells out of pans; cool completely on a wire rack lined with paper towel.

5. TO SERVE: Spoon some strawberries with juices into each shell. Top with ¼ cup yogurt. Spoon remaining berries and juices over yogurt; drizzle with 2 tsp honey and garnish with mint leaves, if desired.

PER SERVING: 171 CAL • 7 G PRO • 32 G CAR • 1 G FIBER • 2 G FAT (0 G SAT FAT) • 3 MG CHOL • 82 MG SOD

Ice Cream Soup

1 pint cherry vanilla ice cream
1 cup fresh fruit mix (such as
   blueberries, halved cherries, and
   chopped peaches and kiwi)

Stir slightly softened cherry vanilla ice cream in a bowl until smooth and creamy.
Pour ½ cup into each of 4 small bowls. Top each with ¼ cup fresh fruit.

PER SERVING: 172 CAL • 4 G PRO • 25 G CAR • 2 G FIBER • 6 G FAT (4 G SAT FAT) • 20 MG CHOL • 41 MG SOD

Fillo Peanut Butter Cups

MAKES 15 / ACTIVE: 5 MIN
TOTAL: 30 MIN

1 box (1.9 oz) mini–fillo shells
   (15 in box)
15 miniature peanut butter cups
   (from a 12-oz bag)
1 can (7 oz) whipped light cream
GARNISH: chopped salted peanuts
   (optional)

1. Heat oven to 350°F. Line a rimmed baking sheet with foil. Place fillo shells on baking sheet.
2. Place a peanut butter cup in each shell. Bake 5 minutes or until chocolate softens.
3. With small metal spatula or knife, flatten and even out chocolate in fillo cup. Let stand at room temperature until cooled.
4. Top each filled cup with whipped cream. Sprinkle with chopped salted peanuts, if desired.

DIFFERENT TAKES
- Instead of peanut butter cups, use Rolos (chewy caramel in milk chocolate).
- Omit whipped cream and top peanut butter cups with a few mini-marshmallows before baking.
- Fill shells with chopped Andes mints instead of peanut butter cups.

PER FILLO CUP: 97 CAL • 2 G PRO • 7 G CAR • 0 G FIBER • 7 G FAT (4 G SAT FAT) • 15 MG CHOL • 36 MG SOD

94   GUILT-FREE SWEET TREATS

Chocolate Fondue

SERVES 16 / ACTIVE: 5 MIN
TOTAL: 20 MIN (INCLUDES
PREPARING DIPPERS)

1 cup heavy (whipping) cream
1 lb bittersweet chocolate, finely
    chopped
2 to 3 Tbsp coffee or hazelnut liqueur
DIPPERS: fresh pear slices, crisp
    ladyfingers, dried apricots,
    marshmallows, strawberries

PLANNING TIP: You can make fondue up to 3 days ahead and refrigerate. Reheat gently in microwave until hot and whisk to recombine just before serving. Rinse and dry fruit up to 2 hours before serving; keep at room temperature. Cut pears just before serving.

1. In a 4-cup microwave-safe bowl, heat cream on high just until steaming, about 1½ to 2 minutes.
2. Add the chocolate; let stand until shiny and softened, about 3 minutes. Add the liqueur and whisk until smooth.
3. Transfer to a ceramic fondue pot or ceramic chafing dish and keep warm over an alcohol burner or votive candle. (You can also use a very small slow-cooker, set on low.) Serve immediately with Dippers.

PER SERVING (WITHOUT DIPPERS): 200 CAL • 2 G PRO • 17 G CAR • 2 G FIBER • 15 G FAT (9 G SAT FAT) • 20 MG CHOL
8 MG SOD

photo credits

CAREN ALPERT > pages 49, 85, 86, 87

IAIN BAGWELL > pages 17, 32, 35, 46, 57, 58, 64, 65, 68, 83, 92, 94

JAMES BAIGRIE > pages 1 top right (and 40), 25, 88

MARY ELLEN BARTLEY > pages 28, 30, 42, 48, 50, 53, 61, 74, 75, 76, 81, 93

JACQUELINE HOPKINS > pages 21, 44, 72 (and 91), 82

FRANCES JANISCH > pages 45, 47, 69, 80

ANASTASSIOS MENTIS > pages 1 bottom right (and 38), 2 (and 34), 6 (and 14),
    15, 24, 54 (and 63), 66, 79, 84, 89, 90

ELLIE MILLER > pages 33, 36, 39, 43, 51, 52, 77

DEBORAH ORY > pages 18, 59

CHARLES SCHILLER > page 10

SHAFFER SMITH > page 78

MARK THOMAS > pages 12, 13, 16, 19, 22 (and 41)

JOHN UHER > page 26

WENDELL WEBBER > page 95

DASHA WRIGHT > pages 1 top left (and 20), 1 bottom left (and 62), 8, 9,
    29, 56, 60, 67, 70, 71